The Schema In Clinical Psychoanalysis

◄ ►

The Schema In Clinical Psychoanalysis

◄ ►

Joseph W. Slap
Laura Slap-Shelton

THE ANALYTIC PRESS
1991 Hillsdale, NJ London

Published by The Analytic Press, Inc.
365 Broadway, Hillsdale, NJ 07642

Library of Congress Cataloging-in-Publication Data

Slap, Joseph W., 1927-
The schema in clinical psychoanalysis / Joseph W. Slap, Laura Slap-Shelton

p. cm.

Includes bibliographical references and index.

ISBN 0-88163-089-6

1. Schemas (Psychology) 2. Psychoanalysis I. Slap-Shelton, Laura, 1956- II. Title

[DNLM 1. Models, Psychological. 2. Psychoanalytic Theory. WM 460 S631s]

RC455.4.S36S53 1991
616.89'17--dc20 DNLM/DLC
for Library of Congress

90-14515
CIP

Printed in United States of America
10 9 8 7 6 5 4 3 2 1

For the Elizabeth Slaps in our lives

Contents

Acknowledgments

I wish to acknowledge the crucial theoretical contributions to this work of Andrew J. Saykin, Psy. D. It was with him and his knowledge of Piaget that I, with my interest in the schema concept and my familiarity with George Klein's (1976) *Psychoanalytic Theory: An Exploration of Essentials*, formulated this model. As his career took a direction in neuropsychology and away from psychoanalytic study and practice, I had to seek someone else as a collaborator when I decided to attempt a book on the schema model. A writer with a knowledge of the pertinent psychological (as opposed to psychoanalytic) literature was needed if the subject was to be treated in the depth required of a book. Carole Malone, Psy.D., agreed to collaborate on this venture. I had been her supervisor during her graduate school days and was greatly impressed by the thinking and energy that had gone into her dissertation. She wrote the proposal that led to the backing of our publisher, The Analytic Press. Regrettably, when her husband accepted a business opportunity overseas she had to give up the project. At this point, Laura Slap-Shelton, Psy. D.,* who had recently graduated from the same clinical psychology program and was long

*While this volume is a collaborative effort and each of the authors is responsible for its contents, Dr. Slap-Shelton made her main contributions in writing the first three chapters. The clinical material was supplied by Dr. Slap; wherever the pronoun *I* appears, it refers to Dr. Slap.

familiar with the schema concept, agreed to work on the book. The program that trained these psychologists was a part of the Department of Mental Health Sciences at Hahnemann University; in the summer of 1988 it moved to Widener University.

I also wish to acknowledge a debt to Joseph D. Lichtenberg, with whom I worked on theoretical issues for many years and coauthored several papers. Our collaborations helped shape my thinking about analysis and led directly to my attempts to find a clinically relevant model. I am grateful as well to Paul Stepansky, Editor-in-Chief of The Analytic Press, who encouraged me to undertake this venture and who provided steady yet nonintrusive guidance throughout. And, lastly, I wish to thank June Strickland, Librarian at the Institute of the Pennsylvania Hospital, for her cheerful and unstinting help.

Preface

For a semester during my second year of residency, I had the good fortune to spend an afternoon a week with Jacob Arlow. For the first hour, Dr. Arlow lectured on psychopathology to the entire group of 12 second-year residents then at Hillside Hospital. He spent the rest of the afternoon, three hours, with a subgroup of four of us. We each presented a case to him for an hour and a half every other week. In other words, he ran four continuous case conferences, and we had the opportunity to hear him discuss and supervise a variety of patients. Although Dr. Arlow has been consistently impressive to sophisticated audiences, he seemed absolutely magical to us at that stage of our professional development. When presenting to him, we often had the experience of his making a comment on how the patient must feel, only to look down at our notes to find that he had anticipated the patient's next remarks practically verbatim.

He stressed the threads or motifs that ran through the clinical material and taught us to listen to our patients in such a manner as to recognize the fantasies that underlay their mental life and repetitive patterns of behavior. His lectures on psychopathology, however, were a much different matter. He was deeply involved with psychic energy concepts and discussed such topics as libido, cathexes, and neutralization. Sometimes there was a spillover of his abstract theoretical concepts into his discussion of the cases we were presenting. At one point in the discussion of a case, he asked a question that telegraphed the answer he was looking for. I have forgotten the question, but the answer I gave was ". . . because it was no longer neutralized." He walked halfway around the conference table—he was standing with a piece of chalk at the blackboard—and clapped me on the back exclaiming, "That's the way to say it!"

While I was flattered by this accolade, I was left with an uneasy feeling. At the break I said to him that of the several ways in which patients had been discussed, he made the most sense to me when he spoke of patients' feelings and fantasies but that I got little out of discussions of psychic energy and other concepts, which seemed abstract and hypothetical. He explained that there were the five metapsychological points of view: dynamic, genetic, structural, economic, and adaptive. During the case discussion, he approached the material from the dynamic point of view, but when lecturing on psychopathology, he stressed the economic and structural points of view.

I was unconvinced. The dynamic and, I add, genetic points of view represented the essence of what had attracted me to dynamic psychiatry. They provided a perspective that treated the patient as a human being with ambitions, hopes, frustrations, and guilt and made understandable his dynamic configurations and repetitive patterns of behavior. The dynamic and genetic points of view, taken together, helped bring order out of chaos and made the task of understanding the patient an activity much like solving puzzles, an activity that has a particular appeal to me. The economic, and certain aspects of the structural, points of view seemed much different. They did not help you understand the patient. Rather, once you understood the patient you might try to fit the material to these points of view. Or if you did not understand the patient, it was often easy enough to come up with an explanation based on the abstract concepts associated with these points of view. Waelder once said of the economic point of view that first you translate the clinical data into economic terms and then when you wish to apply this understanding to the patient, you must translate them back. What is gained by this? he wondered.

As I have said, I had trouble with certain aspects of the structural model. These were the concepts added to the structural model by Hartmann (Hartmann, 1964; Hartmann, Kris, and Loewenstein, 1946, 1949); for example, the ideas that the ego is the sum of its functions and that the superego functions with aggressive energy. Because I never found such concepts useful, I paid them little attention and based my understanding of the structural model on "The Ego and the Id" (Freud, 1923), more particularly on Freud's diagram of the psychic apparatus. The dynamic unconscious was a piece of the ego that had been repressed and was now lodged in the id. It could not become conscious directly and could find expression only through derivatives rising through the preconscious. This version retained the topographic model fairly intact. My thinking that this was a useful way to organize the data found support in a remark by Waelder to the effect that, with the addition of, the idea that defenses were unconscious, he could get along perfectly well with the topographic model. Later, Waelder (1962) was to write that some of the best analysts he had ever known knew next to nothing about metapsychology.

In time, a new problem troubled me. Much of the theory had to do with somatic drives' giving rise to drive derivatives that were shaped or defended against by ego defenses acting at the behest of the superego. Such a model stressed and focused on the seeking out of drive-defense couplings. My patients, however, had issues involving parents, siblings, other relatives, self esteem, gender determination, medical traumata, and so forth; in other words, their dynamics were so rich and complicated that they could not possibly be encompassed by the drive-defense model.

Sometime in the early 1970s I met Joe Lichtenberg at a conference in Washington. Joe had a stack of unfinished manuscripts and asked my help in getting them into shape for publication. He supplied most of the ideas, and I acted largely as critic and editor. We published a number of papers dealing with aspects of defense; one of them, (Lichtenberg and Slap, 1973) on splitting, is occasionally cited to this day. Joe used to say that psychoanalytic theory is "atomized," that so much attention is paid to instincts, defenses, affects, energies, and the like that one loses sight of the forest for the trees. He wished to study larger blocks of material, which he called suborganizations. I was reminded that Schafer (1968) had written of discrepant suborganizations of the mind, by which he meant mental organizations that contained elements which, based on their function, could be assigned to the ego, superego, or id. We settled on the term intersystemic suborganizations.

His ideas about the atomization of psychoanalytic theory and about thinking in terms of blocks of intersystemic material were extremely useful. Moreover, in the course of working with Joe, I became aware that my private version of the structural model was at significant variance with what Sandler (1983) has called the "official theory." It was during this period that I began to think of constructing a model that contained these larger blocks of data and that was free of the many problems I felt were inherent in the structural model. Also at about this time I was serving on the dissertation committee of a graduate student at Hahnemann who took as his topic a comparison of the concepts and developmental timetables of Freud, Mahler, Kernberg, and Piaget. As this student, Andrew Saykin, seemed to have an excellent grasp of these matters, I suggested to him that we try to come up with an internally consistent model of the mind based on the dynamic and genetic points of view. In one of our discussions I brought up the concept of the schema, which I had come across in a paper by Paul (1967) in an early volume of *Psychological Issues*. Saykin responded by speaking of Piaget's usage of the term and the corollary concepts of assimilation and accommodation. I, in turn, was reminded that George Klein (1976) had made much of these Piagetian concepts in his well-reviewed but soon forgotten book *Psychoanalytic Theory: An Exploration of Essentials*.

Turning back to Klein, I was taken with his idea that the dynamic unconscious could be viewed as a nonaccommodating schema, that is, as an organization of the mind that assimilates the data of the external world into its own templates and ignores the differences between the current situation and the past. This concept provided the foundation for a model that

Saykin and I felt had the following advantages: it was experience near; it was able to reconcile or explain such analytic concepts as trauma, repetition phenomena, dream formation, sublimation, transference, developmental lines, and working through; it was based squarely on the dynamic and genetic points of view; and it allowed one to think in terms of organizations at whose core lay traumata and reactive fantasies to these traumata that did not ignore, but rather encompassed, drive-defense interfaces.

Although we were convinced of the superiority of this model, which I employed in my work with patients and in supervision, we soon found that the psychoanalytic community was not receptive. In an attempt to discover the reason for this unpleasant development, I turned to Thomas Kuhn's (1970) *The Structure of Scientific Revolutions*; there I learned that it had taken four centuries for the Copernican discovery that the sun is the center of the solar system to replace the Ptolmaic geocentric model. A good idea will sooner or later catch on.

Papers about the schema model were turned down by the major journals but were accepted by second-line ones. When the ideas were presented at meetings, there was generally some support and the criticisms tended to be varied. I soon realized that part of the difficulty was that, while almost everyone claimed allegiance to the structural model, this apparent unanimity was a pseudoconsensus; actually many different versions of the structural model exist. I arranged to cochair a discussion group on the current status of the structural model at the meetings of the American Psychoanalytic Association and these sessions amply confirmed that there is no clear, internally consistent, widely held understanding of what the structural model is.

Recalling that early on I had been happy with a particular version of the structural model, I returned to that model to see if I could show that the schema model was a derivative of Freud's (as opposed to Hartmann's) structural model and not a competing model. I pointed out that Freud (1915, 1923) made two questionable assumptions about perception in his construction of the structural model: first, whatever his model, he made perception the province of a particular agency through which stimuli must pass before reaching other parts of the psychic apparatus; and, second, he treated perception as a true and exact copy of external reality. In general psychology, this has been called the theory of immaculate perception. When I made the logical changes in Freud's (1923) model, the structural model became roughly congruent with the schema model. The *Journal of the American Psychoanalytic Association* published a paper based on these arguments (Slap, 1987).

Thus, the structural model, as it has evolved under the aegis of the ego psychologists, is in a theoretical cul de sac and does not serve as a guide to clinical work; that is, we have a handed down theory that is not relevant to our practice. Among the consequences of this situation are the following: our institutes teach two virtually separate curricula. Candidates are asked to study the theory in some courses, but they learn to ignore it in clinical seminars and in supervision. Our literature has become repetitious, and analysts pay scant attention to it, perhaps, as Kernberg (1983, personal communication) once commented, because they feel, "Why bother? It has all been said." And lacking a shared working theory, we cannot adequately communicate with one another, a circumstance that has restricted progress in our field.

Undoubtedly there will be readers who feel that they work more or less as I do and that, in my attempt to compare thinking and therapeutic approach as guided by the structural model with that guided by the schema model, the characterization of the former has been distorted. I believe that this perception is bound to occur, because it has occurred in the past and for very good and logical reasons. As I stated earlier, psychoanalysts and analytically oriented therapists have two sets of theory. One set is the official theory of Freud, Hartmann, Kris, and Loewenstein. The other body of theory has to do with what therapists use to guide their clinical work. The model presented here is different from the official theory but often is quite close to how many people work. For many who tolerate this dichotomy in their theory, the ideas presented here will be nothing new; and when I characterize how some therapists work and how many more would work if they took the structural model seriously, they are apt to cry, "But I don't do that! That's a straw man!" I would be most appreciative if, should the expression "straw man" rise to the reader's mind at any juncture in this work, the reader would pause to consider whether he is using as his comparison the structural model as it is represented in the literature or his own way of working with patients.

Joseph W. Slap, M.D.

CHAPTER ONE

◄ ►

Trauma and Neurosogenesis

It is our thesis that psychoneurosis is a manifestation of the activity of a pathogenic organization of childhood residues at the core of which is some traumatic situation or circumstance. The organization, which we term the *sequestered schema*, consists of a central traumatic issue along with reactive fantasies and associated affects. Such an organization may be dormant; if it is active and produces psychopathology, we regard it as a *pathogenic schema*. Insofar as the pathogenic schema is active, relationships and events are cognitively processed according to this template rather than being treated objectively by the more realistic and adaptive part of the mind. In this way, subsequent experience is assimilated by this organization.

Case Illustration

The patient was a graduate student working as an intern in the local office of a national publication. In addition to writing assigned articles, his task was to generate ideas for articles. He thought of doing a story on a new concept in his major field of study. His proposal was accepted, and he was given permission to travel for the purpose of interviewing professionals prominently associated with this concept.

His first write-up was accepted and sent on to the head office. There the editors approved his story with some recommendations for change, which reversed changes he had made at the behest of the local editor. The revised version was accepted by the head office with high praise and without further change. He was informed that, when published, his article would be a lead story.

The patient was elated with his achievement. The following day he was given an assignment that was not challenging (he rated it "middle brow") but found that he was having trouble researching and organizing it. He began to doubt himself. More disturbingly, he began to have regressive feelings (yearning for his mother) that were reminiscent of an incapacitating breakdown he had suffered a few years previously, and he became concerned that he was becoming seriously ill once more. During this crisis it became apparent that the patient had experienced the same sequence of events at the time of his breakdown. He had published an article in a journal that prompted a publishing house to approach him about the possibility of expanding his ideas in a book. He had reacted with jubilation, grandiose fantasies of financial success and fame, inhibition, anxiety, and regression.

The patient's father was a highly placed editor in another national publication. The mother was an intelligent, educated woman who had remained in the home until the children were raised. The patient was the oldest of three boys. From his material it was apparent that the births of his siblings had been severely traumatic for him. He had felt betrayed by the mother for having the babies, and he felt excruciatingly inadequate when he compared himself with his father. He had to contain his rage against his parents and brothers and dealt with his sense of impotence by driving himself to be a superachiever. He had an outstanding high school and college record and went on to the most prestigious graduate school in his field. In high school he had been a varsity athlete and pursued his sport until it became apparent that his physical development was such that he could not hope to compete on a national level.

In this case the pathogenic schema might be outlined as follows: "Father is big and powerful and has a large organ with which he satisfies mother and makes babies while what I have is nothing; I cannot tolerate this, and I will find a way to surpass father and make him weak and inadequate; if I think this or try to do this, I will be severely punished; I had better back off and become a baby again and be close to mother in this way."

Thus we see that this schema was active in his late adolescence and early adulthood; his publishing successes were perceived as the realization of the fantasy that he would become great and powerful and surpass his father; he reacted to this fantasy with a fear of reprisal and beat a retreat by becoming inhibited in his work and ultimately by regressing to a dependent, clinging attitude toward his mother.

Although the patient's material did seem to indicate that the birth of the siblings had been significantly traumatic and had led to the formation of this pathogenic organization, other events, such as primal scene experiences, likely played their role. The patient may or may not have been destined to become neurotic even if no siblings had been born. It is difficult to reconstruct such matters precisely. Nonetheless, for this patient there was the central traumatic issue of abject inadequacy in reaction to which he developed various fantasies that became part of an enduring organization.

What Is Meant by Schema Theory?

In this volume we shall discuss at length the theoretical and clinical relevance of the schema concept in psychoanalytic thought. We do not claim the theory to be original in the sense of our having "discovered" the concept of the schema. The idea of the schema as a psychological entity can be dated back to Bartlett in 1932. Ideas suggestive of the schema model have existed for even longer (Freud, 1895; Janet, 1906). The schema model presented here grew out of a two-fold need 1) to develop a working model of the mind that better fits the clinical data of psychoanalysis, and 2) to create a more parsimonious and consistent theoretical model of the mind than the structural model currently provides.

Psychoanalytic theory has consistently attempted to explain

and describe psychic structures, their genesis, and their role in neurosogenesis. Freud (1923) wrote of the ego's being built out of identifications with significant figures. Since then the concepts of identification, incorporation, introjection, and internalization have been developed to explain the building of various psychic structures. Nunberg (1948) proposed the synthetic function of the ego. Kernberg (1967) wrote of the metabolizing of parental images, and Kohut (1971) wrote of transmuting internalizations as the source of structure building. It is hoped that the schema model, which broadly encompasses these theories, may offer a conceptual organization that brings into relief the features of the concepts of psychic structure and organization relevant to the treatment situation.

Although many psychoanalysts (e.g., Arlow, 1969a; Klein, 1976) have noted the presence of organized and persistent, yet repressed, psychic structures that appear to contain elements of fantasy, memory, and drives, no one has been able to incorporate such organizations into a cohesive psychoanalytic model of the mind. These organizations have been described as film clips that organize a person's perception of current reality along the lines of a traumatic period in the person's life; they have also been called complexes, motifs, templates, scenarios, configurations, and scripts. We are defining pathogenic schemas as organizations of memories, fantasies, theories of procreation and gender determination, primitive defenses, moral values, and other elements that, by virtue of their pressure and activity, give rise to symptoms and other influences on a person's experience and behavior (Slap, 1986). We propose that neurotic behavior results when such repressed organizations interfere with the ego, by which we mean the "dominant mass of ideas" (Breuer and Freud, 1893–1895, p. 116) or the person's integrated perception of self, knowledge, talents, goals, and moral codes. In this chapter we lay the groundwork for a deeper understanding of the schema model and its roots in early and current psychoanalytic theory. We discuss the nature of neurotic fantasy formation with regard to both the concept of trauma and the evolution of the psychoanalytic conceptualization of the psychic apparatus.

Early Theories of Neurosogenesis: Hysteria and the Idea of a Double Consciousness

In the years preceding Freud's initial psychoanalytic theories, physicians, and particularly neurologists, were intrigued with the phenomenology of psychopathology, which came to be understood under the rubric of the hysterias. Many physicians at that time were practicing variations of hypnotism as a means of treating these maladies. This practice led to the observation that many behaviors relating to childhood traumas reappeared during such altered psychic states and that altering the suffering person's level of consciousness at times appeared to bring about an alleviation of symptoms (Bliss, 1986; Breuer and Freud, 1893–1895; Janet, 1906). It was from the study of patients with hysterical symptoms of all types that the earliest theories about the mental apparatus arose. And it was in this period that a major theoretical shift away from purely physiological explanations for psychopathology occurred. Freud is quoted as having said that "Charcot used to say that by and large anatomy has finished its work and the theory of the organic diseases might be called complete; now the time of the neuroses has come" (Gay, 1988, p. 52).

One of Charcot's contributions to the formulation of the understanding and treatment of neuroses was making hypnotism a legitimate medical practice (Gay, 1988, p. 50). Another was the rejection of the idea that only women were hysterical and that the disease was due to a disorder of the uterus. In *Studies on Hysteria*, Breuer and Freud (1893–1895) elaborated their theory of the underlying cause of hysterical symptomatology. There they set forth the famous premise that "hysterics suffer mainly from reminiscences" (p. 7). At this time they were using hypnosis as a therapeutic intervention designed to help the patient remember a traumatic event.

> In the great majority of cases it is not possible to establish the point of origin by a simple interrogation of the patient. . . . This is in part because what is in the question is often some experience which the patient dislikes discuss-

> ing; but principally because he is genuinely unable to recollect it and often has no suspicion of the casual connection between the precipitating event and the pathological phenomenon. As a rule it is necessary to hypnotize the patient and to arouse his memories . . . of the time at which the symptoms first made their appearance [p. 3].

Breuer and Freud reviewed the panoply of hysterical symptoms commonly encountered in the clinical practice of that period, including anesthesias, neuralgias, epilepsy, and narrowed visual fields. They wrote that in some cases the connection between the precipitating event and the pathological behavior is not entirely obvious, but may be symbolic. An example would be having the sensation of nausea secondary to feeling moral reprehension. This symbolic process was considered to occur in the dreams of healthy people. Breuer and Freud introduced the idea that hysteria was analogous to what they termed the traumatic neuroses (p. 5). To the traumatic neuroses were reserved those mental disturbances created by exposure to a situation that created the affect of extreme fear. This fear was considered to be the psychical trauma and was differentiated from the physical trauma of the event. In their view, hysteria could also be explained as stemming from other unpleasant affects: "Any experience which calls up distressing affects—such as those of fright, anxiety, shame or physical pain . . ." (p. 6) may lead to a psychical trauma that may yield symptoms. The trauma need not be a single trauma; it could be the sum of many smaller disturbances acting together.

This idea of a summed group of experiences that produces the disturbed behavior is akin to the concept of the pathogenic schema. The pathogenic schema is considered to be made up of disturbing events or situations and related circumstances, ideas, fantasies, and associated affects; since this organization tends to interpret current life events in accordance with its own template, later life events and relationships are accreted to the pathogenic schema.

Breuer and Freud postulated that the real pathogenic element in these traumatic hysterias was the memory of the trauma, which "acts like a foreign body which long after its entry must continue to be regarded as an agent which is still at work"

(p. 6). They felt that a memory or collection of memories became separated from the main body of ideas and acted independently to create pathology. They described the splitting of consciousness created by the suppression of a memory and the tendency to dissociate as the underlying basis for the manifestation of hysterical behavior (p. 12). Further, once split off from the general consciousness, this idea attracted or came into association with subsequent ideas or experiences, which then also became repressed:

> It turns out to be a sine qua non for the acquisition of hysteria that an incompatibility should develop between the ego and some idea presented to it. . . . The actual traumatic moment then, is the one at which the incompatibility forces itself upon the ego and at which the latter decides on the repudiation of the incompatible idea. That idea is not annihilated by a repudiation of this kind, but merely repressed into the unconscious. When this process occurs for the first time, there comes into being a nucleus and centre of crystallization for the formation of a psychical group divorced from the ego—a group around which everything which would imply an acceptance of the incompatible idea subsequently collects [pp. 122–123].

This conceptualization of neurosogenesis is consistent with the schema theory's understanding that a sequestered schema that contains memories and fantasies related to a traumatic event continues to take in and organize or assimilate new events according to its original infantile organization.

In their "Preliminary Communication," Breuer and Freud described the pathological behaviors as appearing in hypnoid states. In these states ideas were intense, but were cut off from association with the major portion of consciousness. Breuer and Freud indicated that though some patients may have been predisposed to experience these hypnoid states, and thus were vulnerable to dissociative episodes, others acquired dissociative states in response to severe trauma, as well as from difficult and sustained suppression of sexual wishes. The latter two pathogenic factors were described as bringing about "a split-off of groups of ideas even in people who are in other respects unaffected" (p. 12).

Breuer and Freud reported that they were able to cure hysterics by having them recall the traumatic or causative event in a state of hypnosis. In the hypnotic state the patient could be induced to recall the event or events complete with the associated affects. This reexperiencing of the event and its affects allowed the experience to come into association with the general mass of conscious ideas. Once this occurred, the disruptive power of the memory greatly diminished. In "The Psychotherapy of Hysteria" (Breuer and Freud, 1893–1895, pp. 255–305) Freud reported his dissatisfaction with hypnosis as the means of cure, with the central importance of the hypnoid state, and with the separation of hysteria from the other neuroses. He wrote that it was not accurate to consider hysteria as a single entity and that in most cases it was part of a larger neurosis such as an anxiety neurosis or a sexual neurosis (p. 259). He introduced the idea of resistance and censorship, which in all cases of neurosis led to blocked memories and affects. In doing so, he opened to the entire range of psychopathology a single underlying mechanism that could account for disturbances in consciousness caused by the repression of memories, ideas, and fantasies that were in some way related to traumatic or disturbing experiences. An idea that was unacceptable to the ego was defended against by a censorship that denied it access to consciousness. It was the forcing away of the idea that gave the idea its pathogenic power. The very power that forced the idea away was understood to still be in operation when the patient was in therapy.

> The patient's ego had been approached by an idea which proved to be incompatible, which provoked on the part of the ego a repelling force of which the purpose was defense against this incompatible idea. . . . If I endeavored to direct the patient's attention to it, I became aware, in the form of a *resistance*, of the same force as had shown itself in the form of a *repulsion* when the symptom was generated [p. 269].

With the discovery of the resistances, Freud introduced the additional proposal that some aspect of the personality was actually willing this resistance in order to avoid processing the unwanted idea. While the patient may want to be helped, unconscious forces continue to work to prevent unpleasant experiences. This theory set the course for further explorations into the nature of the conscious and unconscious. The role of the trauma in the creation of neurosis had been the key to the understanding of hysterical symptoms. With the understanding that the memory of the trauma, rather than the trauma itself, was the main block in the path of recovery, trauma began to be understood as an external factor that could unleash inner disturbances. The nature of these inner disturbances became a major focus of Freud's work. The importance of reactivating memories by making them conscious led to continued theorizing about the psychic apparatus and the way in which internal and external experiences attained consciousness.

The Topographic Model

The antecedents of the topographic model can be found in Freud's "Project for a Scientific Psychology" (1895). This early model was loosely based on neurophysiological functioning as it was understood in Freud's time. Behavior was defined as the outcome of the attempt to discharge tensions created by inner and external forces. The need to find appropriate means to discharge tension was also a motivational force that generated behavior. Inner tensions were described in terms of psychic energy, which later was understood to be derived from sexual forces and was defined as libidinal energy. If tensions were too great, symptomatic behaviors inappropriate to the environment resulted. By 1896 Freud (1887–1902) had defined the elements of the topographical model. He wrote that memory traces were transcribed several times before becoming conscious. The transcriptions took place at three levels: Perceptual signs (Pcpt.-s), the unconscious (Uc.), and the preconscious (Pc.). Memories were not directly or consciously perceived. They were recorded in the unconscious according to the principle of contiguity in time and then organized by the unconscious into meaningful units. They obtained consciousness by becoming linked with verbal images. The conscious was understood to be a sensory organ that perceived only transcribed information that originated in the unconscious.

With "The Interpretation of Dreams" Freud (1900) introduced the topographic model. The idea of the preconscious was carried over from the model described in "The Project." Also consistent with his early theory was the understanding that new information was initially unconscious and became conscious only after passing through censorships that could disguise disturbing material in such a way that it could emerge in the preconscious and gain consciousness. The psychic apparatus of the topographical theory changed over time. In its final version, before Freud's creation of the structural model, it consisted of the conscious, the preconscious, and the unconscious. At times the conscious and the preconscious were used interchangeably, and at one point the Cs. was assigned to the ego (Gill, 1963, pp. 27, 31, 32). The Pcs, and Cs. were assigned the properties of control of consciousness, motility, affects, some aspects of memory and censorship, and reality testing p. 27). The unconscious was understood to contain two different categories of unconscious material. One was material that remained in the unconscious owing to normal inhibition or repression. The other was material that had been defensively excluded from consciousness and could under certain circumstances attain consciousness (Freud, 1900, pp. 614–615; Gill, 1963, p. 10). Eventually the unconscious became more identified with the dynamic unconscious.

In describing these various structures and the process of transcription of material from the unconscious to the conscious, Freud warned against visualizing them as space-occupying entities. He introduced the idea that images or mental groupings are transcribed through different processes that he described as structures. The concept of mental groupings is consonant with our understanding of a schema of a traumatic event or period. Freud (1900) wrote:

> These images, derived from a set of ideas relating to a struggle for a piece of ground, may tempt us to suppose

> that it is literally true that a mental grouping in one locality has been brought to an end and replaced by a fresh one in another locality. Let us replace these metaphors by something that seems to correspond better to the real state of affairs, and let us say instead that some particular mental grouping has had a cathexis of energy attached to it or withdrawn from it, so that the structure in question has come under the sway of a particular agency or been withdrawn from it [p. 610].

The conscious was privy only to edited versions of reality. When a trauma, such as a sexual assault, occurred, the repressive barriers between unconscious and preconscious were considered to be overwhelmed, causing the ego to be flooded with unmanageable excitation. To maintain energic balance and reduce the level of stimulation, the ego, or, more accurately, the preconscious, attempted to repress information and experiences. Neurotic symptoms arose because of the repression of the memory of the traumatic event, and treatment required that the repressed memory be recalled and made conscious.

Trauma, according to the topographic point of view, depended on the effect of an event on the unconscious. As in dreams, the meaning of the traumatic event was not to be found in the overt and conscious aspects of the event, but rather in the unconscious meaning of the event. Thus, the birth of a sibling may be growth promoting in one child but lead to lifelong psychopathology in another according to the unconscious meaning of the new sibling's birth. Such factors as the age of the child, the degree of the child's preparedness, birth order, and the constitution of the child could influence the nature of the unconscious meaning assigned to this new event. In terms of external traumas experienced in adulthood, Rangell (1967, p. 66) gave as an example of the topographic point of view the various meanings that leaving the army may have for a person; these meanings ranged from the threat of separation, to increased homosexual temptation, to various conflicts organized around the oedipal complex. The type of neurosis engendered would depend on the various unconscious conflicts and fantasies already present in the person.

Libidinal Drives and Neurosogenesis

During the period in which Freud was developing and refining the topographic model he also introduced the theory of childhood sexuality and its role in neurosogenesis. In 1896, he wrote that a disturbance in the sexual life of the patient was always present somewhere in the patient's history. By sexual disturbance he meant actual sexual traumas, which generally occurred between the ages of two and five, in which a parent or other older person either sexually assaulted the child or behaved seductively to stimulate the child's genital zone. It was understood that these experiences could last over extended periods of time (pp. 153–154; Greenacre, 1967, pp. 110–111). According to the topographic model, these sexual experiences were taken in by the Ucs. and not translated to the Pcs. until puberty reactivated the traumatic impressions. Once they were activated, the patient reacted as if the trauma were occurring in the present. Freud described this long-delayed reaction to an early trauma as a "severe posthumous sexual trauma." Even in the case of Anna O, whose hysteria was originally attributed to the stress of nursing her father, Freud felt that an early sexual trauma played a role in creating her neurosis (p. 199; Greenacre, 1967, p. 111). In an 1898 article, "Sexuality in the Aetiology of the Neuroses," he again emphasized the role of sexual experiences and the repression of memories of them at the time of the disturbing childhood events. With "Three Essays on Sexuality" (1905), Freud focused exclusively and extensively on the sexual aspect of early life and the later impact of early sexual experiences. He discussed the infantile amnesias and asserted that an understanding of the forces that bring about infantile amnesia would also bring to light the forces present in hysteria that prevent recognition of certain events and memories (pp. 174–176). In these writings the constitution of the child and the child's proclivity to retain impressions of sexual experiences are related to fixation. The pathogenic effect of early sexual stimulation and trauma were thus ascribed to a combination of the person's constitution and precocity, the tendency to retain early impressions, and the external sexual stimulation itself (pp. 242–243).

In 1906 Freud significantly revised his understanding of the role played by actual sexual traumas. He felt that he had overestimated the actual frequency of such events. He proposed that some of the traumatic events reported by his patients were fantasies of seduction created in order to avoid realization of their own autoerotic experiences. Here the neuroses were clearly attributed entirely to disturbances in the sexual lives of patients, "The etiology of the neuroses comprises everything which can act in a detrimental manner upon the processes serving sexual function" (p. 279). Now the constitutional contribution to neurosogenesis was given primary importance, whereas the accidental sexual traumas were awarded a secondary role. With this formulation, the role of fantasy in neurosogenesis became greater. Hysterical symptoms

> were no longer to be regarded as direct derivatives of the repressed memories of childhood experiences; but between the symptom and the childhood impressions there were inserted the patient's fantasies (or imaginary memories) mostly produced during the years of puberty, which on the one side were built up out of and over the childhood memories, and on the other side were directly transformed into symptoms [p. 274].

With the "Introductory Lectures" Freud (1916–1917) restated his understanding of trauma and appeared once again to place more emphasis on external events. Trauma was described as resulting from a rupture of the stimulus barrier, or protective shield, that kept affects, memories, and fantasies from being registered consciously. The traumatic event was considered to present the mind with too much information over too short a period of time for the psychic apparatus to maintain its equilibrium, resulting in an energic imbalance (p. 275). Greenacre (1967, pp. 114–115) attributes Freud's swing back to recognition of external events as being partly attributable to his interest in the war neuroses resulting from World War I. Freud (1916–1917) noted that the need to repeat traumatic events so as to gain mastery over them—the repetition compulsion—was present in persons experiencing extreme danger and in hysterics alike. In reference to the psychosexual neuroses, he noted that external events were more noxious as the degree of libidinal disturbance or fixation increased. Thus, a reciprocal relation existed between external traumatic events and the sexual constitution in relation to neurosogenesis.

> Are neuroses *exogenous* or *endogenous* illnesses? Are they the inevitable result of a particular constitution or the product of certain detrimental (traumatic) experiences in life? . . . This dilemma seems to me no more sensible on the whole than another that I might put to you: does a baby come about through being begotten by its father or conceived by its mother? Both determinants are equally indispensible . . . As regards their causation, instances of neurotic illness fall into a series within which the two factors—sexual constitution and experience . . .—are represented in such a manner that if there is more of the one there is less of the other. At one end of the series are the extreme cases of which you could say with conviction: these people . . . would have fallen ill in any case, whatever they had experienced and however carefully their lives had been sheltered. At the other end there are the cases . . you would have had to judge that they would certainly have escaped falling ill if their lives had not brought them into this or that situation [pp. 346–347].

He also noted that owing to the immaturity of the child's sexual development, early sexual experiences were more likely to have a traumatic effect (Greenacre, 1967, p. 116).

In "Beyond the Pleasure Principle" Freud (1920) again discussed the cause of trauma as being a rupture of the stimulus barrier secondary to a combination of the intensity of the traumatic stimulus and to the degree of preparedness of the person. If the trauma was a shock, and the ego or the Pcs. (which at times he referred to as the ego) did not have enough time to mobilize energy to prepare for the event, thereby having to undergo the trauma passively, the degree of symptomatology was expected to be greater than if the censorships were prepared to reduce the flow of stimulation to the Pcs. and Cs. The consequences of trauma were considered to be 1) eradication of the pleasure principle, 2) regression to more primitive modes of functioning in an attempt to bind and repress the flood of stimulation, and 3) a loss of energy and efficiency in the psychic apparatus (Furst, 1967, p. 12).

To summarize, the effect of trauma, according to the topographic model, was to flood the unconscious with stimulation too intense for the censorships to prevent the disturbing material from reaching consciousness. Sexual trauma was understood to be the main, if not the only, cause of the neuroses. Originally, this traumatic impression was understood to be the memory of an actual event. Freud then determined that neuroses were often created by sexual fantasies that the child created to prevent awareness of autoeroticism early in childhood. No actual event need have occurred. Gradually, he theorized that there was a reciprocal relationship between the sexual constitution of the individual and external events. Finally, he indicated that, owing to the immaturity of the child, sexual events were misperceived in such a way that ordinary events were experienced as traumatic. This brings us to the introduction of the structural model. Over the period just highlighted Freud had become increasingly aware that the topographic model could no longer account fully for his clinical and theoretical experiences. Internal inconsistencies and discrepancies existed between the model and the behavior of his patients.

Problems with the Topographic Model

In the topographic model, mental contents were located in the different systems according to the property of being unconscious or conscious. Elements organized according to primary process were designated as unconscious; elements organized according to the secondary process were capable of achieving consciousness. As the theory became more developed, the assignment of contents to various parts of the psychic apparatus based on their accessibility to consciousness became increasingly problematic. It was observed clinically that in some patients primary-process material, such as images and sensory experiences, dreams, and certain aspects of symptoms, could gain direct access to consciousness. This was particularly true of contents that were not conflictual. On the other hand, many patients had fantasies that were highly developed and organized according to the secondary process, yet remained inaccessible to consciousness. The location of these fantasies within this system was particularly problematic, in as much as fantasies, especially those of a traumatic and sexual nature arising in childhood, were considered to play a significant, if not determining, role in neurosogenesis (Freud, 1905, p. 226; Gill, 1963, p. 68). We will return to a discussion of the role of fantasy in neurosogenesis later in this chapter. In respect to fantasies and their location in the psychic apparatus Freud (1915c) wrote:

> On the one hand, they are highly organized, free from self-contradiction, have made use of every acquisition of the system Cs. and would hardly be distinguished in our judgment from the formation of that system. On the other hand they are unconscious and are incapable of becoming conscious. Thus *qualitatively* they belong to the system Pcs., but *factually* to the Ucs. . . . Of such a nature are those phantasies of normal people as well as of neurotics which we have recognized as preliminary stages in the formation both of dreams and of symptoms and which, in spite of their high degree of organization, remain repressed and therefore cannot become conscious [pp. 190–191].

Further confusion arose when it became apparent that censorship or repression could not be considered to be a purely conscious process. Although a conscious will was often involved in the patient's avoidance of unpleasurable material, Freud realized that in many instances patients who wished to comply with the command to free associate and not censor thoughts were unable to do so. Further, they were often unaware of their inability to comply (Freud, 1923, p. 17; Gill, 1963, p. 32). Freud (1915) concluded that the only way out of the dilemma was to give up the idea that the criterion of consciousness could serve to differentiate between systems in the psychic apparatus:

> The truth is that it is not only the psychically repressed that remains alien to the consciousness, but also some of the impulses which dominate our ego—something, therefore, that forms the strongest functional antithesis to the repressed. The more we seek to win our way to a metapsychological view of mental life, the more we must emancipate ourselves from the importance of the symptom of "being conscious" [pp. 192–193].

The Structural Model

With the structural model, Freud (1923) attempted to resolve the difficulties presented by the topographic model. Given the failure of the use of conscious and unconscious as major ways of organizing clinical data, he created a new system that was intended to avoid this issue. In the new model, the ego was introduced as one of the three structures of the psychic apparatus. It was defined as possessing the conscious and all the properties attributed to the Pcs. and Cs., as well as the perceptual system. In addition, the unconscious repressing forces were also located in the ego. The id was described as the reservoir of instinctual, chaotic psychic energy, which operated according to the pleasure principle and had no judgment. The ego was considered to have developed from the id, and material that was not acceptable to the ego was described as being repressed to the id, where it formed part of the dynamic unconscious. Whereas in the topographic model perceptions were taken in by the unconscious and then transcribed before becoming conscious, in the structural model it was the ego that took in information. The id had no access to this information except as it was introduced to it by the ego. It was the role of the ego to bring the reality principle to bear on the id (Freud, 1923, p. 25).

The superego was introduced as a third structure, representing the moral values or conscience of the psychic apparatus. The superego was an outgrowth of the ego and was described as forming after, and as a result of, the oedipal phase of psychosexual development. The superego contained idealized identifications with the parents and was a reaction formation to the early powerful, id-dominated wishes and fantasies about the parents (pp. 55–59). Unconscious feelings of guilt and need for punishment were attributed to the superego. Freud noted that it was not possible to localize and define the superego in the same way that the ego and the id were defined. Because of its close relationship to the id impulses, the superego was described as paradoxically placing the ego under the sway of the id (pp. 36–37).

The efficacy of the structural model in resolving the problems posed by the topographical model is discussed in Chapter Six. Here we note that Gill (1963, pp. 47–48) remarked that the same confusion about how to determine the location of various mental contents continued to persist with the structural model because of its formula that all three agencies of the psychic apparatus now contained a part of the dynamic unconscious. Arlow (1969a, b) also indicated that fantasies pose a problem for analytic theory in that their contents resemble conscious mental thought in their organization, inner consistency, and freedom from self-contradiction and yet remain unconscious.

The understanding of the role of trauma changed to some degree with the advent of the structural model. As mentioned earlier, the repressive barriers now came from the side of the ego. The ego had to maintain a balance between the libidinal and aggressive drives of the id and the punitive and repressive forces of the superego. Neurosis was no longer understood as a conflict between unconscious and conscious forces. And trauma was not understood as being the moment of repudiation by the Pcs. Intersystemic conflict now took on the central role as the cause of trauma in the neuroses. Such conflict could be secondary to internal and external factors. Rangell (1967) wrote, "The increasing intersystemic tension results in increasing strain that, when its intensity reaches beyond a certain threshold, can become a traumatic stimulus" (pp. 73–74). Disturbing memories and fantasies could reemerge at any time to create overwhelming internal tensions.

With "Inhibitions, Symptoms and Anxiety" Freud (1926) greatly broadened the scope of the meaning of trauma as an etiological factor in neurosis. As he continued to explore the internal causes of neurosis, he used the terms "anxiety trauma" and "traumatic situation" to refer to situations in which lack of gratification and more benign experiences of being helpless lead to the build-up of unmanageable amounts of stimulation. He differentiated automatic anxiety from signal anxiety. Automatic anxiety was considered to be the initial reaction to a real and on-going danger situation. It involved the autonomic nervous system and physical fear reactions. While appropriate for mobilizing the body to react to dangers that may have been present in the individual's early life, it represented an inappropriate reaction to later life situations, which generally do not require flight or fight response.

Signal anxiety, on the other hand, represented a more mature warning system in which the ego responded to the threat of danger in order to avoid a traumatic situation. Danger was defined as a state of ego helplessness in the face of too much internal or external stimulation or both. Freud felt that in the infant one of the first signs of the presence of signal anxiety occurred when an infant responded with anxiety to the absence of the mother after having recognized her as a protective agent. Thus the automatic anxiety associated with real danger became displaced onto a threat of a danger situation: "mother not here." Freud felt that the initial fear of not having mother near was the precursor for anxiety associated with other fears of loss, such as loss of mother's love, castration, and loss of the superego's love (Furst, 1967, pp. 13–14). In general, signal anxiety was felt to be a healthy mechanism that allowed the mental apparatus to avoid or prepare for a potentially traumatic event and to achieve mastery over such an event. But signal anxiety could become pathological and symptomatic if the ego incorrectly estimated a situation as being a danger situation on the basis of memories of earlier experiences. In such cases, conflict between the structures of the mind could lead to neuroses.

With the advent of the theory of signal anxiety, the scope of the concept of trauma had been widened. The role of the ego became broadened to include the perception and anticipation of traumatic events, and thus its functioning depended not only on its past experiences but on its ability to utilize them to gauge current and future situations correctly. Freud (1926) referred to the "traumatic situation" to describe the state of helplessness engendered when the ego was unable to maintain a homeostatic balance. Repetition of the event was understood as a means of gaining mastery by turning passive into active:

> Let us call a situation of helplessness of this kind that has actually been experienced a *traumatic situation*. . . . Taking this sequence, anxiety-danger-helplessness (trauma) we can now summarize what has been said. A danger situation is a recognized, remembered, expected situation of helplessness. . . . The ego, which experienced the trauma passively, now repeats it actively, in a weakened version, in the hope of being able itself to direct its course. It is certain that children behave in this fashion towards every distressing impression they receive, by reproducing it in their play. In thus changing from passivity to activity they attempt to master their experiences psychically [pp. 166–167].

The increased focus on internal sources of stress further highlighted and emphasized the significant role of fantasy in neurosogenesis. The scales of the reciprocal balance between constitution and environment again tilted heavily toward the constitutional endowment of the psychic apparatus. A strong ego was considered an indication of ability to avoid most traumatic intersystemic conflicts, even those stimulated by external situations. External situations were considered to be relevant according to their effect on the intersystemic balance within the psychic apparatus.

Important early figures were considered in terms of their ability to satisfy or allow the expression of the infant's and young child's drives. Little attention was given to the contribution of the parent's behavior to neuroses, and reports of sexual traumas were increasingly interpreted as fantasies related defensively to libidinal drives. Another change in the understanding of neurosogenesis, and one that eventually led to much confusion, was that now, with the structural model, trauma or the anticipation of trauma could be generated from any portion of the psychic apparatus. Pathogenic fantasies and behaviors were to be interpreted in terms of the roles of the psychic structures—the ego, superego, and the id—rather than in terms of their more direct relation to early childhood experiences that became distorted over the years and continued to influence perception of adult life events.

The complexity of the interrelation of these early perceptions was often at risk of being lost to the task of fitting isolated experiences into a model of conflict among the structural components of the mind. For example, it now became possible to focus on superego guilt caused by aggressive wishes toward the father while missing the concurrent aspect of the early traumatic constellation that involved other significant figures and circumstances of the traumatic period. For example, feelings of abandonment by the mother, inadequacy, and rage at a new sibling may come together to create a script that is repeated throughout a person's life as new people are incorporated into the original early roles. While the importance of the early memories and fantasies was appreciated, the structural model failed to account fully for their place in the psychic apparatus and their relationship to neurotic behaviors (Arlow, 1969a, b; Gill, 1963). The schema model, we submit, offers a way of conceptualizing the psychic apparatus that accounts for the power and activity of these early memories and fantasies generated by early traumatic events.

In "Fetishism" (Freud, 1927), "Dostoevsky and Parricide" (Freud, 1928), and "Specialist Opinion in the Halsmann Case" (Freud, 1931) there appears to be a greater balance between constitutional and external traumatic factors in the genesis of abnormal behavior. For example, in discussing the origin of fetishism, Freud (1927) wrote that the fetishist's choice of a fetish is in part the result of a traumatic amnesia in which the last event before the actual traumatic event becomes the source of the fetish (see also Greenacre, 1967, pp. 120–121). In regard to Dostoevsky's epilepsy, Freud (1928) stated that an underlying organic weakness provided pathways for disturbances due to physical imbalances in the brain's chemistry and for others due to imbalances in the psychic apparatus leading to intensified brain activity. He wrote, "The epileptic reaction is also undoubtedly at the disposal of the neurosis whose essence it is to get rid by somatic means of excitation which cannot be dealt with psychically'' (pp. 179–192). The death of Dostoevsky's father preceded and, according to Freud, precipitated the onset of full epileptic fits at the age of 18. In the Halsmann Case, Freud (1931) rejected the idea that the Oedipus complex alone led to the murder of the father by the son. Instead he felt that the effects of shock and the related disturbance in memory were not given enough weight in the case.

In ''New Introductory Lectures'' Freud (1933) discussed birth trauma as the prototype of signal anxiety. The traumatic situation here is again a situation in which the psychic apparatus is unable to discharge intense and painful tension.

In ''Moses and Monotheism'' Freud (1939) integrated his understanding of the role of trauma and the role of psychosexual development in a much quoted passage summarizing his theory of neurosogenesis. He wrote:

> We give the name of traumas to those impressions, experienced early and later forgotten, to which we attach such great importance in the etiology of the neuroses. . . . All these traumas occur in early childhood up to about the fifth year. Impressions from the time at which a child is beginning to talk stand out as being of particular interest, the periods between the ages of two and four seem to be the most important; it cannot be determined with certainty how long after birth this period of receptivity begins. . . .
>
> These three points—the very early appearance of these experiences (during the first five years of life), the fact of their being forgotten, and their sexual-aggressive content—are closely interconnected. The traumas are either experiences on the subject's own body, or sense perceptions, mostly of something seen or heard—that is, experiences of impressions . . . [pp. 75–76].

He further noted that there are two paths to coping with these traumas. The first he identified as an active process in which fixation to the trauma leads to attempts at repetition of the trauma in order to remember and relive it. The reenactment of the trauma is an effort to gain mastery, to make passive into active. This process can lead to the establishment of more or less permanent character traits. The second process was described as a passive one in which extreme efforts are taken to forget the trauma. This process leads to defenses aimed at the avoidance of elements that can be associated with the trauma and eventually to phobias and inhibitions. Both trends are present in the symptom formations seen in the neuroses.

This passage—with its clear emphasis on the early sexual experiences of the child which in effect form the backdrop for traumatic impressions that are then kept alive in efforts to master or, alternatively, reject them—represents the final development of Freud's understanding of neurosogenesis. The balance between constitutional and external sources of trauma remains tilted slightly toward the constitutional or developmental side in this final formulation. Greenacre (1967, p. 127) noted that the wish or fantasy content of the child's thinking was thought to be the main source of traumatic conflict and the actual stimulating event was practically incidental. Klein (1976) wrote, "In the development of psychoanalytic theory the possibility of traumatic events or encounters became obscured by the conception of trauma as an exclusively intrapsychic event being traumatic solely in relation to an internal representation of conflicting aims" (p. 188). Greenacre (1967) suggested a working definition of trauma that gave more weight to the role of external events. She did not limit her definition to events related to sexual drives but, rather, spoke of traumatic conditions as "any conditions which seem definitely unfavorable, noxious, or drastically injurious to the development of the young individual" (p. 128).

Klein (1976) proposed that there were two varieties of traumas: nonconflicting and conflict-involved traumas. In the first category he placed traumas related to being in a situation in which active coping is not possible, leading to feelings of being "passively overwhelmed." He wrote, "In such cases the person feels a profound helplessness, a feeling . . . that nothing he could do or desist from doing would avert the danger to which he is forced to respond" (p. 188). He noted that different situations were perceived as dangerous and overwhelming according to the developmental phase of the child. In the category of conflict-involved traumas he included experiences that, because of their relatedness to already established internal conflicts, were perceived as traumatic and induced further conflict. He pointed out that in this instance some events would have greater meaning for one person than for another because of the difference in accumulated internal experience (pp. 188–189).

With the development of ego psychology by Hartmann (1958, 1964) came a greater emphasis on the role of the ego in mastering traumatic or conflictual material. Along these lines, Solnit and Kris (1967), speaking from an ego psychology point of view, distinguished between shock trauma and strain trauma. They defined shock trauma as having certain criteria, including that an internal or external demand leads to an overwhelming of the ego's adaptive functioning. An overwhelming stimulus had qualities that included being sudden, disruptive, penetrating the stimulus barrier, and creating autonomic dysfunction and psychic regression. Efforts at repetition and mastery were not successful and led to further trauma. Strain trauma was defined as demands to which the ego was sensitized but had not fully mastered. They might be mastered through further attempts and repetitions.

The schema model proposes a simpler definition of trauma and may account for several varieties of experience, including that of being helpless and overwhelmed, of being shocked, and of the impingement of reality on the common psychosexual fantasies of childhood. The model can encompass these various notions of trauma because its central proposition is that all these aspects may or may not be included in the schematic representation of the traumatic event. The traumatic element is considered to be any event that cannot be integrated or accommodated into the main body of ideas. The roles of internal fantasy, conflict, and external factors are not mutually exclusive. Indeed, one cannot be understood without understanding the others since the events and figures involved in the original psychic disturbance contribute the cast of characters and dramatic line for future enactments of the traumatic situation in later life. The fantasies and conflicts of the person shape the perception of objects and situations and determine the rhythm, pace, and emotional pitch, as well as the overall structure of the drama.

Development and Neurosogenesis

Further exploration of the role of psychosexual development in the formation of neurosis will be useful at this juncture. Freud specified the period between two and five as the time when many lasting traumatic impressions are experienced. He also indicated that childhood fantasies are built upon early impressions and that this conglomeration becomes repressed en masse as an internal structure that remains unintegrated with the rest of the person's experiences. Klein (1976) wrote:

> His [Freud's] ideas of the causes of hysteria changed in time, but one assumption persisted: that a structural residue of the past (at first assumed to be an actual seduction experience, later an erotic fantasy, later a wish) persists as a selective organizing principle of behavior and thought. [p. 164].

The lack of integration of this repressed collection of memories and fantasies (which the schema model understands as repressed or sequestered schemas) strongly influences the behaviors and motivations of the person. Again, quoting Klein, "Throughout the changes of emphasis in psychoanalytic thinking, the most invariant principle has been that the structures guiding action originate in attempts to resolve breaches of integration" (p. 165).

What is it about this period of development between the years of two and five that leads to traumatic experiences that are later repressed? Freud (1939) wrote of the need for a constitutional or maturational readiness before certain external or accidental experiences can be realistically assessed. Fenichel (1945) proposed that whether or not an event becomes traumatic depends on the degree to which it reactivates latent or preexisting conflicts. Greenacre (1967), rejecting the idea that only the instinctual drives and the incipient fantasies about the infantile sexual experiences lead to traumatic impression, suggested that the maturational striving of the child leads to efforts to seek out experiences. These experiences add to and color the initial age appropriate fantasy. She wrote:

> In the pre-oedipal years and later there is a maturational pressure that will generally cause the child to reach out and utilize the slightest opportunities for experience, if these are not readily supplied spontaneously. The child then creates or supplements that which is not easily given him. But under conditions short of absolute deprivation, the child himself may act as the seducer. He may get little response and suffer frustration, or he may attract a response which, in intensity and content goes beyond whatever are his specific needs at the time [pp. 127–128].

This concept is similar to Piaget's (Piaget and Inhelder, 1969) understanding that children seek out stimulation of all sorts as part of their normal development. The results of their explorations form the core of their experience, and the level of their perception determines in part the meaning that will be given to their explorations. In Greenacre's (1967) view, the degree to which objects such as parents and siblings interact purposefully or accidentally to reinforce the underlying age-appropriate fantasy will determine to what degree the fantasy becomes an important factor in the individual's personality:

> . . . the basic fantasy will always be a fusion of the genetically determined instinct representation with whatever responding stimulations the environment has to offer. These may reinforce the endogenous elements in the nuclear fantasy, or may tend to counteract them . . . the greater participation of the external elements in the early experience usually results in stronger and more diversified sensory or sensual components [p. 129].

In the same vein, Arlow (1969b,) wrote that "young children regularly intermingle their perceptions of reality with wishful fantasy thinking and sometimes find it hard to distinguish in recollection between what was real and what was imagined—between what constituted fantasy and what constituted accurate memory'' (p. 35). He wrote of the central importance of these fantasy–reality constellations or schemas in determining the perceptions and behaviors of patients:

> External perception and internal fantasy were intermingled at the time of the experience and together they formed the reality which to the patient was the record of his past. It was upon this confused fantasy thinking, which was dynamically effective in so many aspects of his life that the inner eye of the patient remained consistently focused [p. 43].

Illustrating this principle, Greenacre (1967, pp. 131–132) presented the case of a woman who at the age of two years (in the anal phase of development) had happened to hear strange noises coming from her parents' bedroom one night while she was on the way to the bathroom. She had entered the room to see what was happening and was confronted with a scene of confusion and excitement with bloody things in the bathroom and in the bed. After some improvement in the patient's overall level of functioning had been achieved in the course of treatment, a symptom came to light involving a disturbance in her ability to have bowel movements. She required absolute privacy and often had to distract herself from awareness of her activity by reading. If she was unsuccessful in her attempt, she resorted to an enema. This disturbance began with her first mature sexual experience. Greenacre was able to trace the components of the disturbance to several common fantasies involving magical and omnipotent ideation that were strengthened by, and organized according to,the central disturbing event of her second year.

The fantasies associated with the various phases of psychosexual development are well known (Freud, 1905) and provide a means of understanding the maturational or developmental phases that young children pass through. The work of Piaget is another guidepost in understanding the conceptual and perceptual abilities of young children. Through his (Piaget, 1926;

Piaget and Inhelder, 1969) careful delineation of the cognitive life of children, Piaget demonstrated that children actively seek out new experiences.

Other researchers into infant and toddler behavior have also pointed to the very active role of the young child in guiding its own development. Their findings have brought into question some of Freud's basic assumptions about childhood development and provide support for the idea that young children actively seek stimulation and experience according to their maturational capacity. For example, evidence indicates that the model of drive discharge or tension reduction as the motivating force behind all behaviors of the infant and young child does not explain the need for an optimum level of stimulation (Lichtenberg, 1983; Stern, 1985). Lack of stimulation is not an ideal, but it can serve as the basis for aberrant behaviors initiated to provide the necessary level of stimulation for an optimal homeostasis. Another area in which Freud's original concepts have been challenged recently is the proposal that the infant's motivation for forming object relations is entirely due to the need to fill instinctual drives, the original drive being that of hunger. The findings of many researchers suggest that infants are born with unique, innate capacities to perceive both persons and objects and to interact effectively and actively with the caregiver (Bornstein, 1984; Lichtenberg, 1983; Stern, 1985; Wolff, 1966). As Lichtenberg (1983) has observed, "The neonate emerges as an organism whose responsiveness is centered on and geared to a perceptual-motor-affective dialogue with the mother" (p. 6).

Given the heightened appreciation of the active role that cognition plays in guiding the behavior of infants and young children, it is necessary to incorporate these findings into a consistent theory of neurosogenesis. Piaget proposed two overarching principles that govern cognitive development: assimilation and accommodation. These processes will receive further attention in Chapter Three; for the present it will suffice to note that in the assimilation of an event the experience is recorded and perceived without affecting the child's understanding of events in such a way that growth or adaptation to a new experience occurs. In contrast, accommodation refers to a process in which an experience is perceived and processed so that growth occurs. The new experience adds to and changes previous ways of perceiving an event or object and leads to more mature functioning. The schema theory proposes that in a similar fashion, fantasy formations such as those described by Arlow (1969a, b) and Greenacre (1967) are schemas of experience in which assimilation prevails over accommodation. In the case of the adult who suffered the traumatic discovery of her mother's miscarriage, this event was assimilated according to the normal perceptual abilities of the two-year-old child; because of its disturbing and confusing nature, however, it was never accommodated or integrated into the course of her otherwise unremarkable development. It remained repressed or sequestered and continued to have an activity of its own that interfaced with her otherwise mature level of functioning.

Clearly, instinctual drives and pressures shape the fantasies found at the different phases of psychosexual development. Yet the child's ability to take in new experiences—that is, to understand complex sequences, verbalizations, affective displays, and intentional behaviors—is greatly influenced by the level of the child's cognitive development. The years specified by Freud (1939) as being peculiarly suited for the creation of traumatic impressions have also received considerable attention from Piaget. According to Piaget and Inhelder (1969), at the age of two the child begins to be able to form and use symbols to represent people and objects that are not actually present. Children at this time begin to lose their embeddedness in motor and sensory activity and come to perceive others as separate from themselves and their activity (Kegan, 1982). The development of the symbolic function is sequential, beginning with imitation of a model after the model is no longer present. Next comes a period of symbolic play in which pretending becomes possible. Then follows drawing. Next comes the formation of a mental image that is an internalized imitation. The sequence culminates in the ability to use language to indicate events that have occurred in the past (Piaget and Inheider, 1969, pp. 53–54).

During the period from two to four or five years, children operate or create their symbol systems in a highly individualized manner. Children in this phase of development are considered to be in Piaget's preoperational phase. In this phase, rules of logic do not apply. Instead, children create symbols that they endow with highly personal meanings. These symbols are assimilated directly into mental schemas representing different experiences. Ginsburg and Opper (1969) wrote, "With this form of interaction the child can assimilate the external world almost directly into his own desires and needs with scarcely any accommodation. He can therefore shape reality to his own requirements" (p. 81). This form of thinking was defined by Piaget (1926) as egocentric. He described perception in this phase of development as being syncretic with events remembered in loosely connected and disorganized wholes.

This description of the cognitive processes of the young child suggests that the child is unable to perceive and interpret correctly the complexities of adult sexual behavior and the meaning of many complex events. Additionally, because of the automatic tendency to incorporate perceptions into preexisting, highly personalized mental representations, children in effect are living in a world in which fantasy predominates. As basic schemas of early experiences are laid down, they shape the toddler's perception of future events. With the maturation of the latency period, the cognitive processes of the child become increasingly ruled by logic, and accommodation begins to come into balance with assimilation. Many of the child's early experiences are later accommodated and remain accessible to consciousness. More disturbing experiences, however, are likely to remain unaccommodated.

The schema model proposes that these assimilated but not accommodated disturbing experiences, which are highly endowed with fantasy and idiosyncratic meanings, remain active but unconscious. They remain active by continuing to assimilate new experiences according to the anachronistic, highly personalized meaning of the original experience, thereby altering perception and preventing a fully adaptive response to average life events. Because of their distorting influence on perception and their inhibition of adaptive behaviors, the schema model labels such schemata pathogenic.

Summary

In this chapter, the history of Freud's conceptualization of the role of trauma was traced throughout his writings. The issue of where the balance lies between the effect of external and internal stimulation in creating neurosis was a constant theme. Initially, Freud felt that real external traumatic events of a seductive or sexual nature left memory imprints that later led to the disorganized behaviors observed in the hysterias. He later recognized the role of fantasy in shaping memories of events and in creating disturbances in functioning.

With the advent of the structural model, the early importance of whether mental contents were conscious or unconscious (the topographic model) gave way to a model in which various contents were assigned to three agencies of the psychic apparatus, all of which had unconscious elements. Internal and maturational events gained primacy in the causation of neurosis. The role of fantasy in neurosogenesis was also increasingly recognized. But the location of fantasy content in the psychic apparatus of the structural model was unclear. With "Moses and Monotheism," Freud (1939) presented an integrated picture of neurosogenesis that highlighted the years from two to four as those in which traumatic events leading to later pathology occurred.

While Freud delineated the nature of fantasy appropriate to the phases of psychosexual development, he did not have access to careful research into the cognitive abilities of infants and young children. Research by Piaget and others suggested the presence of a phasic developmental path for cognitive growth. Further, their researches indicated that infants and young children actively seek out experiences and object relations. The period of time Freud believed to be so essential to the development of the neuroses corresponded to the period of cognitive development Piaget termed preoperational. Cognition in this period is characterized by the beginnings of a primitive symbol system in which perceptions are directly assimilated to previous experiences and organized according to highly personalized meanings. Virtually no accommodation occurs during this phase. According to the schema model, events occurring during this time period are more likely to be misperceived and at the same time are less likely to be accommodated. With maturation, the majority of early mental schemas laid down during this period are gradually accommodated to a more realistic and adaptive schema, the ego. However, the more disturbing and confusing events are likely to remain unconscious and unaccommodated. The schema model proposes that these disturbing events continue to assimilate new material to themselves and continue to affect perception in such a way that symptoms and conflicts derived from early disturbing or traumatic events emerge in the course of an otherwise well-adapted adult life.

CHAPTER TWO

◄ ►

The Schema Concept in Psychodynamic Theory

The schema concept has a long history that dates as far back as the work of Janet (1906) who summarized his views on integrated subsystems of the mind as follows:

> An idea, the memory of an event, for instance, the thought of a ferocious animal, the thought of a mother's death, all these form groups of psychological facts closely connected with one another. They are certain kinds of systems comprising all sorts of pictures and all sorts of tendencies of certain movements, but with a strong unity. These systems in our minds have their strength and their laws of development that are peculiar to them. They have also a great tendency to development when they are not kept within bounds [pp. 40–41].

Janet wrote that pathology occurred when one or more subsystems became separated from the greater mass of ideas and became unaccessible to consciousness. He observed that in such patients behaviors appeared to be driven by these now unconscious but organized systems of memory, affect, and motor tendency.

Later the concept of the schema was developed by cognitive psychologists, notably Piaget (1926) and Bartlett (1932). Recently, the schema concept has been given more attention in cognitive and psychoanalytic theory. In this chapter, we review the use of the schema concept in these fields and discuss the relation between these various uses and the schema model presented here. The schema model is a description of how the mind afflicted by neurosis and, by extension, other functional disorders, is organized. It enables the clinician to organize the data the patient brings to therapy in a clinically useful way. By viewing patients' material as being manifestations of underlying sequestered schemas and by adapting Piaget's concepts of assimilation and accommodation, the theory invites close inspection of these cognitive processes; it does not claim a fundamental knowledge of the complexities of these processes nor can it account for the biophysical (or constitutional) factors in psychopathology. Further work, both theoretical and experimental, is needed in all these fields. It is hoped that the schema model, by providing a new paradigm, will lead to new investigations and discoveries within psychodynamic science and, further, that it will provide bridges to other fields.

Piaget (1926; Piaget and Inhelder, 1969) introduced the concept of the schema as a key feature of his theory of intellectual development in early childhood. Essential to this theory was the process by which new information is taken in and added to previously learned knowledge, that is, the process by which schemas are modified and adapted to the external world. Piaget and Inhelder described this process as one of assimilation and accommodation; in differentiating this theory of cognitive growth from the behavioral associational theories, they wrote:

> . . . reality data are treated or modified in such a way as to become incorporated into the structure of the subject. In other words, every newly established connection is integrated into an existing schematism. According to this view, the organizing activity of the subject must be considered just as important as the connections inherent in the external stimuli, for the subject becomes aware of these connections only to the degree that he can assimilate them by means of his existing structures. In other words, associationism conceives the relationship between stimulus and response in a unilateral manner: S $\longrightarrow$ R; whereas, the point of view of assimilation presupposes a reciprocity

> ⟶ R, that is to say, the input, the stimulus, is filtered through a structure that consists of the action-schemes (or, at a higher level, the operations of thought), which in turn are modified and enriched when the subject's behavioral repertoire is accommodated to the demands of reality. The filtering or modification of the input is called *assimilation*; the modification of internal schemes to fit reality is called *accommodation* [pp. 5–6].

Piaget's theory as it relates to the schema model is discussed in greater detail in the next chapter. For now it is important to note that Piaget's theory represents a dynamic cognitive understanding of perception and its role in building mental structures. In contrast to the structural model, which views perception as a photographic representation of reality accessible to only certain parts of the mind, Piaget's model provides a deeper understanding of how external reality is processed.

In Piaget's theory, motivation is understood to derive from a natural process of seeking to maintain an equilibrium between assimilatory and accommodatory processes and to maintain a unified and coherent psychic organization. Thus, in his theory, the inborn and ongoing process of psychic growth itself serves as a major motivating factor for behavior.

> Indeed, the sentiments involve incontestable hereditary (or instinctive) roots subject to maturation. They become diversified in the course of actual experience. They derive a fundamental enrichment from interpersonal or social exchange. But, beyond these factors, they unquestionably involve conflicts or crises and re-equilibrations, for the formation of the personality is dominated by the search for a coherence and an organization of values that will prevent internal conflicts (or seek them, but for the sake of new systematic perspectives. . .) [Piaget and Inhelder, 1969, p. 156].

In a similar way, the schema model posits the need to maintain psychological equilibrium as a motivating factor of the ego in both neurosogenesis and in the attempt to get well through insight-oriented therapy. As the motivations, perceptions, and behaviors of the sequestered or pathogenic schema are understood and integrated into the main mass of ideas or ego, greater psychic integration is achieved. However, the motivations of the sequestered or pathogenic schema are understood to be directly linked to the traumatic event, situation, or period and to efforts to recover from it. The schema model does not posit an encompassing motivation for human behavior.

The schema model is consistent with Bartlett's (1932) description of the schema. His theory conceived of the schema as an integrated organization of past experiences, both perceptual and behavioral. He defined the schema as

> an active organization of past reactions or of past experiences which must always be supposed to be operating in any well-adapted organic response. Whenever there is any order or regularity of behavior, a particular response is possible only because it is related to other similar responses which have been serially organized, yet which operate not singly as individual members coming one after another, but as a unitary mass [p. 201].

Such organizations of memories, fantasies, affects, and modes of response, whether normal or maladaptive, suggest the psychoanalytic concept of the complex. The repressed unconscious, too, is an organization of memories, fantasies, affects, motives, and other elements, which meets Bartlett's definition of schema. Bartlett indicated that the unitary schema was made up of subschemata that interacted with one another but were relatively independent. He described schemas as being interconnected and organized in a hierarchical fashion such that the activation of one set of schemas could be moderated by the activation of other sets of schemas. In this fashion, he believed, memories consisted of the overall sum of the various schemas associated with a particular event or person. Similarly, the schema model posits that the ego functions in such a way that experience is represented and processed in a realistic and consistent manner. The sequestered or pathogenic schema, by reason of its lack of connection with the healthier core, tends to function according to its own template rather than being modified by the experience of reality; it does not profit from feedback.

The concept of the schema has been employed in several more recent cognitive theories of information processing to describe mental organizations that process perception, affect, and behavior. These theories tend to ignore motivational issues and focus exclusively on cognitive processes that may account for clinical and experimental data. Segal (1988) writes that in the field of depression research, "schemata consist of organized elements of past reactions and experience that form a relatively cohesive and persistent body of knowledge capable of guiding subsequent perception and appraisals" (p. 147). Taylor and Crocker (1981) use the schema concept in their research on social cognition. Cantor and Mischel (1979) and Cantor, Mischel, and Schwartz (1982) write that individuals build prototypic models for categorizing others and situations and that the more characteristics a person or situation has that match a particular schema, the more likely the person or situation is to be stereotyped (in Piagetian terms, assimilated) to the schema. Some studies indicate that in many instances schemas persist despite the addition of new information; they address, that is, a tendency for assimilation to prevail over accommodation. Westen (1988), in a paper that integrates information-processing theory with psychodynamic considerations of transference, remarks that "old schemas never die" (p. 107). He suggests that the more generalized and less specific the schema, the more difficult it will be to change and that in understanding transference reactions it is important to determine from what level of generalization, or where in the organizational hierarchy of schematic representations, the transference reaction is generated. Another type of schema theory is that of the mental script; Abelson (1981; Schank and Abelson, 1977) writes about scripts as schemas of sequences of actions and social interactions that may often operate on an unconscious level.

Beck's (1967, 1976) cognitive theory of depression relies on the construct of negative self-schemas as part of the psychic structure of the depressed patient. In his model, early negative self-experiences lead to the formation of an organized collection of negative self-concepts, which in later life may be triggered consciously or unconsciously by events reminiscent of the childhood experiences. Kovacs and Beck (1978) write that depressogenic schemas "organize those aspects of the person's experience that concern self-evaluation and relationships with other people . . ." (p. 529).

Segal (1988), in a review of experimental support for the existence of an underlying self-structure or schema in Beck's theory of depression, indicates that academic research techniques have not always been successful in demonstrating the existence of cohesive underlying cognitive structures. Drawing on the work of Higgins et al. (1977) and Tulving and Pearlstone (1966), he suggests that a corollary explanation for underlying structures is construct accessibility/availability theory, which holds that the more often a construct is activated, the more easily it is accessed. In terms of the schema model, the activity of the pathogenic schema may be understood to be to some degree attributable to the confluence of new events assimilated by this structure.

Schemas are also understood to be accessed through affect. Affect is said to increase accessibility to mood-congruent information (Bower and Cohen, 1982; Isen, 1984; Blaney, 1986; Segal, 1988). Conversely, Fiske (1982, in Westen, 1988), proposes that new situations which elicit old schemas also bring forth the affect associated with the schema. She called this phenomenon "schema-triggered affect." These two concepts taken together suggest a circular feedback system in which affect stimulates a pathogenic schema, which in turn continues to misinterpret new information, thus maintaining the affect.

The schema concept has appeared in recent psychoanalytic theorizing. As noted in the previous chapter, the structural model does not account for the organization and the central role of unconscious fantasy (Inderbitzin and Levy, 1990). There is also dissatisfaction with Freud's treatment of perception (Schimek, 1975; Slap, 1987; Linnel, 1990). Inderbitzin and Levy (1990) note that the concept of unconscious fantasy "has not been developed and refined as psychoanalytic theory evolved over time" (p. 114). They see a problem in the "difficulty in finding a place within our current theories . . . for dynamically repressed mental content, particularly when such content regularly appears to have an enduring and crucial impact on subsequent mental life'' (p. 117). They review three trends in current psychoanalytic thinking about unconscious fantasy: Arlow's explanation in terms of the structural model, Sandler's explanation in terms of both the topographic and structural models, and the schema model (Slap, 1986; Slap and Saykin, 1983, 1984), which they describe as a ''microstructural system of the mind'' (p. 119). They conclude that unconscious fantasy plays a central role in mental life. While they attribute fantasizing to the ego, they agree with Beres and others who reject the notion of structure-specific fantasies, that is, ego, superego, and id fantasies. Rather, they view fantasies as intersystemic, adding that clarification results when the act of fantasizing is differentiated from the products of that activity. They describe the fantasies themselves in a manner that is consonant with the schema model:

> [fantasies] have a stable and enduring quality, indicating some degree of structuralization. They organize psychic reality, influence subsequent perception, experience, and behavior, and become guiding forces for future pathological as well as adaptive compromise functions. They embody important childhood instinctual conflicts, and their repression during the oedipal period due to conflict leads to relative sequestration from the reality ego [p. 126].

Arlow (1969a, b) wrote of the activity and manifestations of unconscious fantasy. In Arlow's (1969a) terminology, the sequestered schema is called ''fantasy thinking'' or ''fantasy system'':

> The perceptions of reality are sensed against the background of individual experience. Memory, recording [sic] conflicts, traumata, vicissitudes of drives, and of development are organized in terms of the pleasure–unpleasure principle into groups of schemata centering around childhood wishes. These make up a continuous stream of fantasy thinking, which is a persistent concomitant of all

> mental activity and which exerts an unending influence of how reality is perceived and responded to. . . . The organized mental representations of this stream of inner stimulation is what I call fantasy thinking. It includes fantasies and the memory schemata related to the significant conflicts and the traumatic events of the individual's life [p. 29].

Yet, Inderbitzin and Levy (1990, pp. 118–119) fault Arlow for, among other problems, failing to provide an understanding of how fantasies from the past affect perception and behavior and for bypassing mental content with his emphasis on defining structures as groups of functions.

Schafer (1968) wrote of "discrepant suborganizations of the personality" and gave as an instance the fetishist's knowing and not knowing the anatomical distinction between the sexes:

> . . . this distinction must not be seen as two isolated,small-scale phenomena; they are, in fact, expressions of two antagonistic organizations of motives, mental processes, and representations . . . the fetishist's not knowing the distinction indicates an organization of castration fantasies and anxieties, homosexual wishes, superego structures, and constriction of reality-testing processes through defensive displacement, symbolization, repression, avoidance, and denial . . . [pp. 98–99].

Klein (1976) uses the term schema in describing organized mental systems. He writes of psychoanalytic theory from a Piagetian point of view, and, as noted in the Preface, his work served as a crystallization point in the development of the schema model. Relevant to the schema model is his discussion of repression. He begins by stressing that Freud's original theorizing about repression did not involve a drive model. Rather, as noted in the previous chapter, "the first and central elements of neurosis were psychical trauma and conflict among ideas, and the consequences for behavior of conflicting ideas" (p. 240). He writes that much of the clinical significance of the concept of repression has been hidden by energic and otherwise metapsychological theories of cathexis and consciousness. He attributes this confusion to the nature of Freud's early theory-making and to the failure to integrate a more experience-near treatment of cognition into the model. Klein (1976) describes the repressed as an unconscious schema having the power to influence behavior without the individual's awareness of its activity:

> In contrast to intentional thought, thought related to a repressed schema precludes responsiveness to information concerning its meaning. In Piaget's terms, such a train of thought is assimilative but not accommodative; it is impervious to change by feedback. . . . The results of such assimilation without accommodation of feedback is *gaps in the person's comprehension of the significance for the self of an acted-upon idea* [pp. 244–245].

Klein describes the "self-schema" and the "meaning schema." He sees the self as a "central apparatus of control" and schemas as cognitive records of experience. In defining what he means by the concept of the schema, he stresses that his focus is on the experiencing person rather than on a theoretical system. Klein does not discard the ego when speaking of the schema but defines the self-schema as a grade of ego organization. The self-schema is a structure, built through many experiences, that makes possible the maintenance of self-identity. He writes, "From the first emergence of a self-schema, preservation of its identity and continuity is a prominent organismic concern" (p. 280). He conceptualizes the self-schema as developing as the infant gradually becomes able to differentiate which experiences are generated by its activity and which come from external sources. Klein shifts the focus of the significance of anxiety from a signal of anticipated danger if certain drives are not repressed, to a manifestation of the disruption of the unitary self. From his vantage, trauma is defined as any event that disrupts the sense of self-unity.

In a similar vein, Stolorow and his collaborators (Atwood and Stolorow, 1984; Stolorow and Lachmann, 1986) have developed a structural approach to the understanding of psychoanalytic experience in which the self replaces the ego as the center of activity; the self is considered to consist of structures of experience. The self structure, in their view, is closely and reciprocally related to the activity of the person and his interactions with the environment: ". . . we assume that recurrent patterns of conduct serve to actualize . . . the nuclear configurations of self and object that constitute a person's character" (Atwood and Stolorow, 1984, p. 34). Structures may be conscious or unconscious, depending on their fit with the overall self-schema; thus, repression is a negative organizing principle and the unconscious is

> that set of configurations that consciousness is not able to assume, because of their association with emotional conflict and subjective danger. . . . Particular memories, fantasies, feelings, and other experiential contents are repressed because they threaten to actualize these configurations [p. 35]

These configurations, which are analogous to the sequestered and pathogenic schemas we describe, are understood to be activated and suppressed according to the nature of the affective interpersonal experience they encapsulate. They are assumed to arise in an intersubjective context in which allowable and unacceptable emotions are initially defined by the environment, with subsequent internalization of the limits of acceptable affects.

Wachtel (1980) suggests that Piaget's concepts of the schema and assimilation are pertinent to the understanding of transference. He writes that transference reactions may be understood as the activity of schemas in which assimilation predominates over accommodation. One of the advantages he cites for making use of these concepts is that they eliminate a false distinction between psychic reality and reality proper, and that they make more precise the meaning of current interactions for the patient. Thus, events in therapy may not be accurately perceived, since aspects of the relationship with the therapist lead to the activation of old schemas. He suggests that, in addition, this process may occur outside the therapeutic situation; this latter point is consistent with the well-recognized phenomenon of extraanalytic and (extratherapeutic) transferences. In terms of the schema model, we would say that transference is ubiquitous as a consequence of the activity of sequestered and pathogenic schemas.

The work of Horowitz (1971, 1977a, 1988) has evolved with the aim of redefining psychodynamic theory in terms of cognitive as well as dynamic processes. He (1988) uses the schema concept to describe various microstructures within the personality. The self-schema is "a view of the self whose conscious representation is not necessarily available but persists unconsciously to organize inner mental processes" (p. 29). He distinguishes the self-schema from the self-concept, which is entirely conscious, while using the term self-organization to refer to "the summation of all a person's self-concepts and schemas at various levels of conscious and unconscious processes" (p. 29). Thus, according to Horowitz, there are multiple self-schemas, including motivational schemas, relational schemas for different types of relationship, and body schemas. Self-schemas may be superordinate and thus organize other self-schemas, or they may be fragmented into partial self-schemas.

He uses the schema concept clinically as a way to understand the cognitive and dynamic aspects of the patient's representation of self and objects and as a way of understanding various mental states and transference experiences of the patient. For example, in discussing the splitting process of borderline personalities, Horowitz (1977) describes a patient who fluctuated between sets of self–other schemas, including "trustful learning child" coupled with "ideal interested parent" and "defective evil-dirty child" linked with "ideal disinterested parent" (p. 551). In addition, he notes the presence of a realistic self-schema that was often overwhelmed by the others and thus unable to integrate these structures. Horowitz feels that these various schemas work in isolation and do not influence one another, a circumstance upon which he comments as follows: "[the] extreme capsulations are probably the result of arrests in psychological development" (p. 552). In discussing the personality and analysis of an hysterical patient, he describes several types of self-schemas exhibited by the patient as well as impairments in cognitive functions, including perception, representation, association, and integration, which preserved the overall repression of various self and other schemas. He describes the influence of her schemas in a manner consonant with the schema model's understanding of the assimilatory nature of sequestered and pathogenic schemas.

> Her self- and object-schemata at the outset of analysis concretized an internalized version of these familial patterns into a set of stereotyped roles. These roles . . . were imposed compulsively on every relationship. Real experiences were held at such great distance by nonappraisal of meanings and by general denial. These stereotypes were perpetuated rather than revised [p. 355].

Also similar to the schema model (see Chapter Eight) is Horowitz's rejection of the concept of a true or real self. While Horowitz (1989, personal communication) agrees with the authors of this work that his and our models are fundamentally different despite the common use of the schema concept, he agrees that various subschemas are understood to exist in a relatively integrated and organized manner, which accounts for variability and adaptability, as well as continuity, in human behavior and personality manifestations.

To summarize, both cognitive and psychoanalytic theorists have used the schema concept in various ways. They have in common the idea that psychic organizations exist that are not normally available to conscious awareness yet affect perception and behavior. Psychoanalytic writers understand that schemas which interfere with effective daily functioning have their origins in early childhood. Klein and Wachtel make use of Piaget's concept of the schema and its assimilatory and accommodatory activity. The schema model elaborated in the following chapters differs from those of Klein, Stolorow, Atwood, and Lachmann, and of Horowitz in that it does not propose a multiplicity of self-schemas along with discrete partial or subschemas. Instead, the schema model avoids such closures, while conceptualizing the sequestered and pathogenic schema as consisting of all the aspects of feeling, behavior, perception, and motivation that were associated with a traumatic period and were not integrated by the adaptive, realistic ego. This is not to say that under certain circumstances some aspects of these schemas may not be greatly emphasized or isolated, giving the schemas a compartmentalized character. Further, the schema model differs from those of Piaget, Klein, and Stolorow with respect to the issue of motivation. Those theorists understand the need to maintain psychic homeostasis to be a primary source of motivation for human behavior. According to the schema model, motivation, as far as the sequestered or pathogenic schema is concerned, is best understood in terms of the traumas suffered by the person and the efforts made to recover from or compensate for them.

CHAPTER THREE

◄ ►

The Schema Model

The Unitary Schema or Ego and the Pathogenic Schema

In the previous chapters we discussed neurosogenesis and reviewed the use of the concept of the schema. We showed how this concept is far from new and how it was simultaneously but separately developed by both psychoanalysts and cognitive psychologists. In this chapter we present and discuss the schema model as it is applied in psychodynamic practice. In advancing this model, we include some concepts associated with earlier models of the mind. In particular, we borrow from the work of Piaget to explain how certain organized memories and fantasies remain sequestered from the main mass of ideas or ego. As we discuss this model, it will be necessary to stipulate some terminology and perhaps justify it. This model has relatively few concepts; nonetheless, we believe it provides a valid framework with which one can organize and deal clinically with psychopathology in its considerable complexity.

We view the mind as consisting of two major organizations, the unitary schema, or ego, and the pathogenic schema. By unitary schema, or ego, we refer to what Breuer and Freud (1893–1895) identified as the "dominant mass of ideas." The unitary schema is that part of the mind that consists of many schemas, loosely linked and integrated with one another and relatively accessible to consciousness. The schemas are considered to be organizations that include memories, affects, perceptions, factual knowledge, cognitive style, and other elements. They are based on past experience but are modified by new experiences and form the basis for adaptive behavior.

While schemas are representational structures, they also provide the basis for activity, both perceptual and motor. This concept is similar to Janet's understanding of the psychologically healthy person (see van der Kolk and van der Hart, 1989, p. 1532), whom he described as having a coherent memory system in which unified memories of the totality of perceptions, emotions, and actions related to a certain experience are available for conscious awareness as needed. Horowitz (1988) describes several types of schemas that he considers to be the units of psychological functioning. These include body schemas, self-schemas, interpersonal schemas, and working schemas, among others. In our model many such types of schemas are considered to exist in a fairly unified matrix and thus would be included in our conception of the ego. Bartlett's (1933) description of a schema as "an active organization of past reactions or of past experiences which must always be supposed to be operating in any well-adapted organic response"(p. 201) and which organize behavior by acting together in a unitary mass fits our concept of the ego. The model is also congruent with Piaget's (1926) conception of the mental apparatus as consisting of increasingly integrated and differentiated schemas that function flexibly in unison to determine the organization of new behaviors (Wolff, 1960, pp. 21–22).

We use the term ego rather than unitary schema or some other term because this term, particularly in its prestructural usage, is familiar and approximates in meaning the unitary schema. We feel that this understanding of the ego fits well with our clinical experience of how patients function and perceive. The ego is that aspect of the patient that is adaptive and reality oriented. It is that aspect of the patient that the therapist, for the most part, addresses as he seeks to help the patient gain insight. It is the part of the patient that grows in the course of treatment as the pathogenic organization is delineated, exposed, and worked through. It consists of that fairly well-organized collection of past experiences that have been successfully assimilated and accommodated. Depending on the nature of the pathology, the patient may have a highly cohesive and integrated ego or a more diffusely organized one.

The second organization in this essentially bipartite model is the sequestered schema. It is organized around traumatic events and situations in childhood that were not mastered and assimilated, but instead remain latent and may or may not give rise to overt symptomatology, although they may influence behavior by affecting choices and awareness. We label the sequestered schema whose activity causes distress or symptomatology or is in any way disruptive to the life of the patient, the pathogenic schema. Pathogenic schemas are active mental organizations that contain traumatic impressions, fantasies, and affects. Unlike the schemas of the ego, the impressions and fantasies that make up the pathogenic schema derive from previous experiences that were painful and overwhelming. Because of the traumatic nature of these experiences, awareness of them and integration into the ego have not been possible. They continue to exist, often in unmodified form, as freeze frames of past situations or events, unchanged by gains in maturity and understanding. The pathogenic schema is roughly equivalent to the dynamic unconscious. Thus, in the course of therapy (or in the course of a person's experience), when pathogenic schemas do become available to inspection, they appear unreal, primitive, childlike, and disturbing. This concept of the pathogenic schema is close to Janet's description of "subconscious fixed ideas," which are described as ideas that organize the "cognitive, affective, and visceral elements of the traumatic memory while simultaneously keeping them out of conscious awareness" (van der Kolk and van der Hart, 1989, p. 1532). Janet described subconscious fixed ideas as arising from highly emotional and damaging previous experiences from which the patient has attempted to dissociate himself.

Early Childhood Development and the Pathogenic Schema

Assimilation and Accommodation

In Chapter Two, we reviewed some theories of early development that make use of the schema concept. Here we shall attempt to integrate these theories into a more coherent description of how pathogenic schemas arise. Piaget's model of the mind is characterized by two main functions: organization and adaptation. Organization refers to the tendency to systematize one's actions, perception, and thoughts. Adaptation refers to the two complementary processes that operate on an ongoing basis: assimilation and accommodation. As discussed in Chapter Two, assimilation is the modification of perceptual data to fit preexisting psychic structures or schemas. Accommodation is the modification of internal representations or schemas to fit reality. Adaptive cognition requires a process of both assimilation—the incorporation of the new experience as if it were a familiar experience—and accommodation—modification of schemas to adapt to what is novel about the experience.

Piaget posits a "need to function," which results from a disequilibrium between assimilation and accommodation. The need to function refers to the child's efforts to seek out the experience or stimulus that has created the disequilibrium in order to accommodate to it. Once accommodation has occurred, the child is free to move on to a new experience. For example, when a child seeks to master eating with a spoon, he repeatedly attempts to use the spoon by himself and demonstrates serious application of his energies to its mastery. Once he has created the necessary motor accommodations to manage the spoon easily, his attention and interest abate and he moves on to new experiences.

Using Piaget's formulations, we view the core of neurosis as arising when the child is confronted with an experience to which he, despite repeated efforts, is unable to accommodate. This experience and the attempts to deal with it constitute the root of a separate organization left behind as the ego develops. Once sequestered in this way, such schemas are not affected by later experiences. The person is unaware of the schema, which remains active but unconscious. In George Klein's (1976) words, since the schema is not amenable to correction by feedback, it leads to ''unthinking behavior'' (p. 297). This new schema formation, because it is unconscious, remains relatively unaltered by new experiences, and the disequilibrium between assimilation and accommodation is maintained. In terms of Piaget's distinction between maturation and learning, the pathogenic schema matures; that is, it develops by assimilating experiences to itself but does not learn. It does not change in structure in order to adapt to new experiences and conditions. While such assimilation may change the content of the repressed schema to varying degrees, the ''plot'' tends to be resistant to change. The new data of experience are perceived and reacted to in the distorted, anachronistic manner dictated by the unaccommodating or pathogenic schema. The ego and the pathogenic schema are both active in perceiving and processing new experiences; the latter are parallel processed (Horowitz, 1977). Thus, whatever the individual thinks or experiences is the resultant of forces of the ego and the pathogenic schema.

The Repetition Compulsion and the Schema Model

Freud (1920) attributed the repetition of maladaptive behaviors in disturbed persons to the repetition compulsion. He stated that once repression of an instinctual wish or impulse has occurred, any new experience that stimulates a similar impulse, even if the experience is not in itself threatening, will lead to further repression. Owing to this automatic repression, certain categories of experience remain sheltered from the processes of the ego. He considered the repetition compulsion to be the ''fixating'' factor in repression. The schema model accounts for the repetition compulsion in terms of the resistance of repressed schemas to change. This resistance accounts for repetitive phenomena, what has been described as id resistance, and for the persistence of the effects of childhood experience into adult life. When a patient is analyzed to the point where the repressed pathogenic schema is understood, the schema seems to pervade the analytic data. All is seen to be influenced by these core ideas, and the life of the patient can be comprehended, as noted earlier, as a play or motion picture being constantly remade: the plot is supplied by the repressed schema; the settings, props, and actors keep changing as the patient goes on through the years.

Though repressed schemas seem not to change, they do, in fact, change slowly through the years. There are similarities and differences between the infantile neurosis that constitutes the original version of the schema and the adult and transference neuroses, which are later versions.

Although he did not employ the concepts of schema, assimilation, and accommodation, Freud (1926) did take up the question of changes in the repressed schemas over the course of time:

> With regard to the repressed instinctual impulses . . . we assumed that they remained unaltered in the unconscious for an indefinite length of time. But now our interest is turned to the vicissitudes of the repressed and we begin to suspect that it is not self-evident, perhaps not even usual, that those impulses should remain unaltered and unalterable in this way. There is no doubt that the original impulses have been inhibited and deflected from their aim through repression. But has the portion of them in the unconscious maintained itself and been proof against the influences of life that tend to alter and depreciate them? In other words do the old wishes about whose former existence analysis tells us, still exist? The answer seems ready at hand and certain. It is that the old, repressed wishes must still be present in the unconscious since we still find their derivatives, the symptoms, in operation. But this answer is not sufficient. It does not enable us to decide between two possibilities: either that the old wish is now operating only through its derivatives, having transferred the whole of its cathetic energy to them, or that it is itself still in existence too. If its fate has been to exhaust itself in cathecting its

> derivatives, there is yet a third possibility. In the course of the neurosis it may have become re-animated by regression, anachronistic though it may be now. These are no idle speculations. There are many things about mental life, both normal and pathological, which seem to call for the raising of such questions [p. 142n].

The Organization of the Pathogenic Schema

Thus far we have described the major organizations of the mind and the formation of the sequestered schema. Although we have indicated that the sequestered schema is a freeze-frame of the period in which it developed, we have not explored its organization. Because sequestered schemas are generally formed during the period from the second to the seventh years, their organization is characterized by the cognitive style of that age period. Piaget's (1926) description of the cognitive functioning of this age group, which he referred to as the preoperational stage, as being egocentric contributes to our understanding of the difficulties encountered by the adult neurotic whose activities are partially driven by the pathogenic schema.

By egocentric thought, Piaget meant that the child is unable to view a situation from more than a single perspective. For a child of this age, activities are important only for their effect on the child. The child is just beginning to develop language and to develop the ability to think symbolically. In this phase, the child takes in experiences largely through assimilatory processes. New events are recorded in chronological approximation rather than according to a more sophisticated organizational template. Thus, unrelated events may become significantly linked in the child's mind by way of a highly personalized symbol system. The child relies heavily on past events to interpret new events. In addition, the child assumes that he or she has understood verbal communications even when this is not the case. Instead, the child has taken in the language and assigned it a likely meaning. Often children of this age group will repeat bits of things that are told to them with little apparent understanding. Ginsburg and Opper (1969) refer to this stage of thinking as "a case of assimilation gone wild" (p. 110). In addition, many of the events that the preoperational child experiences are too complex for full verbal encoding. Given this description of the child's mind at this time, it may be inferred that schemas formed during this period contain motoric and affective memory traces as well as illogical verbal narratives.

With egocentric logic, children create schemas of personal, often idiosyncratic relationships between themselves and external reality and the symbols (or signifiers) that represent them. Normally children will attempt to gain mastery of new experiences to accommodate them through their interactions with the environment. But children who experience such an event as the birth of a sibling, a particular parental relationship, or a separation as an overwhelming circumstance may not be able to accommodate the event. As described earlier, such situations lead to the formation of schemas that are not integrated by the ego, but instead become sequestered or repressed. Thus, the assimilatory nature of the pathogenic schema is often two-fold. First, it is internally organized so that assimilation predominates over accommodation. Second, by nature of its sequestering from the more adaptive functions of the ego, the pathogenic schema does not partake in cognitive development that would adapt it to current circumstance.

To give some idea of the processes we are discussing, consider the following examples. The child who views his or her parents in the act of coitus might feel that mother is being hurt by father because the mother is moaning and the father appears to be attacking her. The anger that the parents may express if they discover that they are being observed is also taken into the experience and adds to the child's affective memory. Even if later the parents explain that what they were doing was loving, the young child may have difficulty reconciling his or her own already sequestered schema of the event with the parents' explanation. If activated later in life, the schema organized around this event could lead to a maladaptive interaction with the environment.

Another example is the child whose mother goes to the hospital to have a baby. Despite preparation, the child may still encode the experience as "mother's abandoning me and leaving me alone" rather than as "mother's temporarily leaving home to have a baby." As this is the kind of reasoning that characterizes the child during those years in which infantile neuroses arise, it is not surprising to find that such reasoning characterizes the organized residues of childhood.

Case Illustration

A middle-aged woman suffering severe back and neck spasms of psychophysiological origin entered treatment in an agitated, depressed state. The patient was an only child. Her father was a self-made millionaire with a reputation for ruthlessness in business affairs. He ruled the home with an iron hand; the mother was subservient, and the patient was expected to be the same. It became evident that she was guilty over, and defended against, intensely held wishes to castrate (or kill) the father and take possession of his power. She was constantly being manipulated by men: refusal of their demands, however unreasonable, had the unconscious meaning of castrating them; guilt over such fantasies forced her to give in to their demands.

The set of thoughts or fantasies that lay at the core of her repressed material is as follows: Father is big and powerful. Mother is terrified of him. He is different from mother because he is a man and has a penis and has a job and makes money. I wish I could be like him and not be a nothing like mother. I wish he would take me to his office and show me how to be like him. But if he did I might not be able to do it; after all, I am just a little girl. But he does not take me, or show me—he treats me the way he treats my mother. I hate him and wish he would die. Some day I'll show him. I'll be big and important and he will be a nothing. This is a terrible way to think. I am bad and deserve to be punished by him.

Each of the elements in this set of thoughts can be amply illustrated from the analytic material. For some period, the patient was phobic about visiting her parents at their condominium in an exclusive Florida resort. She was expected to sit around the pool with her mother and the other ladies. She also developed severe anxiety at certain women's luncheons she was obliged to attend. Such situations stirred the feeling, which she abhorred and defended against, that she was just a stupid, know-nothing woman like the others.

During the course of the analysis the patient returned to school and earned her bachelor's degree and a master's degree. She was extremely anxious about papers, presentations, and examinations, even after she established her ability to handle the work. (She graduated *summa cum laude*.) She was afraid that instructors and fellow students would see that she was just a stupid girl. She constantly felt that she did not have *it*, something she lacked and felt that the more capable students had—although she was not able to say what *it* was. During a practicum at an agency that was having difficulties both with funding and maintaining its work load, the patient became conflicted over fantasies of exposing the shortcomings of the director and seizing control of the agency upon graduation. Another derivative of the "I'll show you—some day I'll be big and you will be nothing" was the recrudescence of her agitated depression when it appeared that her father would be removed from the board of a philanthropic organization as a consequence of embarrassing, erratic behavior and she would be named in his stead.

At this point it may be worthwhile to bring up a point in psychoanalytic theory that appears paradoxical and is potentially confusing. On one hand, we are given to understand that the "unconscious" is characterized by fluidity; it uses unbound energy and employs primary process; on the other hand, we are given to understand that the repressed is quite fixed, perhaps unalterable. The length of analyses is in part explained by the resistance to change of the content of repressed material. One need only recall Freud's (1937) remarks about the fixity of penis envy in women and castration anxiety in men. In accordance with the schema model, we agree with the position that the unconscious is characterized by fixation. We understand fluid, primary-process mental phenomena to be interface phenomena; that is, primary-process mentation arises as a product of conflict between the ego and repressed material. Such an argument could be the subject of a separate volume and cannot be gone into exhaustively here. We do, however, wish to make the point that the same mechanisms that are attributed to the primary-process thinking characteristic of the unconscious are also attributed to dream work and to the defensive organization, both functions of the ego.

Psychic Conflict

In the topographical model, psychic conflict was described as existing between the drive and defense. In the structural model, the ego, id, and superego were the macrostructures, and conflict was felt to result when the ego was in conflict with either or both of the other parts of the psychic apparatus. In the schema model, there are two distinct types of conflictual interface. One is the interface between the ego and the pathogenic schema. The other conflictual interface lies within conflictual material of the pathogenic schema. In the course of treatment, it is important that the therapist be sensitive to the difference between the two interfaces. This point is amplified in the following chapter.

CHAPTER FOUR

Clinical Exposition

There is a very funny line in *Cyrano de Bergerac* (Rostand, 1897) that exemplifies how a person sensitized to a particular issue, in this case Cyrano's feelings of inferiority associated with his nose and what it may symbolize, will tend to perceive events in his current life as though they pertained to this issue. In terms of the schema model, we would say that the sequestered schema assimilates the event, or, in other words, perceives it , according to the template of a pathogenic residue of the patient's childhood. The line occurs in Act II at a point when the cadets in Cyrano's company warn the new recruit, Christian, about Cyrano's sensitivity. One of them admonishes, "Would you die before your time? Just mention anything convex . . . or cartilaginous . . ." (p. 121).

In a similar vein, a young attorney was extremely sensitive to any situation that could be perceived as his being displaced by a young rival. When he was two years old, the patient's mother required a hospitalization of several months following an auto accident. He reacted poorly to this separation and was unfriendly to his mother when she returned. She soon became pregnant and delivered a brother, whom the patient despised. Another brother, born a few years later, was better tolerated by the patient.

After the birth of the first brother, the child was trapped in a painful situation for which he could not find a resolution. His brother was there to stay, and his rage at this sibling and at his parents for having him was not acceptable to his parents and engendered guilt and fears of punishment. He was unable to resolve the matter, and the configuration of traumatic distress, fantasies of murder and punishment, and associated affects of anger, fear, and remorse remained as a separate organization within the patient's psyche and constituted a freeze-frame of this period in his life. The activity of this organization in processing events and relationship in his adult life was abundantly clear.

When given the files of several law students who were applying for summer positions in the firm for which he worked, the patient left them in the locker room of his squash club. He had been impressed with the background and achievements of these prospects and felt that he would be overshadowed were they to join the firm. When he was asked if he would mind if a space he intended to move into were given instead to two paralegals who worked closely with a partner in an adjacent office, he created a storm that hurt his standing in the firm. When a junior associate complained about an assignment that would encroach on what would otherwise have been a long holiday weekend, the patient became enraged and screamed at the complainer, calling him, among other things, a spoiled brat. When the entire city was excited about the local team playing in and winning the World Series, the patient secretly rooted against them; they were, after all, everyone's darlings. When his wife became pregnant, he dreamed of encountering a stranger in his favorite childhood play spot and fighting with him.

In another instance, a little girl strove to win her father's love, attention, and respect while feeling despair at his exclusive interest in her younger brother, whom the father seemed determined to mold into a perfect male. She harbored resentment against her brother but defended against it, fearing that her father would despise her if she were mean to the boy. Years later, now an art history doctoral candidate, she was attracted to a homosexual male professor. She strove to win his love, attention, and respect while recognizing that his preference was for males. Indeed, it was known that he had provided several thousand dollars of personal funds to enable a favored male student to do research in Italy. She was teaching a course on women artists and, to meet the requirement that one's teaching be evaluated, invited this professor (she could have chosen any faculty member) to observe her class. She wished desperately that the class would go well. At a point late in the class, the patient called on the only male student taking the course, as he had not contributed to the discussion up to that point. The student was not able to answer the question he was asked, and the patient was horrified by the thought that she had embarrassed him and that the professor would be enraged at her for doing so. The class ended, leaving the student shaken in spite of the professor's smiling and making a thumbs up gesture as he left.

The parallels with the childhood situation are clear. She was making a presentation to her professor who, like her father, preferred boys. The content of the course, as the patient pointed out, was designed to show that women and men alike were valuable. She thought that she had hurt the male student qua brother and that the professor would punish her. As it turned out, the professor rated her highly, sought to arrange a teaching award for her, and was particularly complimentary about the tactful way she had handled the male student.

These vignettes illustrate how painful, unresolved situations of childhood remain with people as organized residues; they constitute freeze-frames of the traumatic period. Insofar as they are active, they shape the perception and processing of current situations and relationships. Thus, the situation in which newly graduated lawyers were admitted to the firm was perceived as baby brothers coming into the family; and the opportunity to teach a class while being observed by an admired professor had the meaning of proving to father that girls were valuable too. If we accept that neuroses are organized in this way, it follows that there are two distinct kinds of conflictual interface. One kind has to do with the interface between the realistic, adaptive part of the mind—which might be called the ego or the dominant mass of ideas (Breuer and Freud, 1893–1895) or the unitary or self-schema (Klein, 1976)—and the pathogenic residue taken en bloc. The other type of conflictual interface is within the pathogenic, or sequestered, schema.

To take the example of the lawyer, in the original situation the birth of the brother was experienced as an overwhelming narcissistic blow. The child had to deal with feelings that he was regarded as less valuable than this newcomer and with dangerous wishes to get rid of his rival, wishes that had to be scrupulously controlled. These wishes and the need to control them constituted one kind of conflictual interface. In order to get along in the family, he was forced to adapt to the situation, which he did by pushing it aside en bloc. When asked, his parents claimed that they did not remember his being particularly resentful of his siblings. This pushing aside (or sequestering or repressing) created the second kind of interface, that between his realistic and adaptive ego and the painful and unresolvable situation.

The recognition that there are these two kinds of interface is crucial to organizing the data of cases and in carrying out treatments. Let us turn to another case, one that will be discussed extensively.

A man in his late 20s was referred by the analyst he had been seeing when he came east to enter professional school. He suffered inhibitions that impaired his functioning in romance, business, and athletics, areas for which, by virtue of his appearance, intelligence, charismatic personality, and physical gifts, he had an excellent but unrealized potential.

His neurosis was a freeze-frame of the fifth year of his life, when his mother delivered his only sibling, a brother. Because of circumstances surrounding the birth, the survival of the brother was for a while in grave doubt. The patient's care was handed over to a housemaid while the greatest attention was paid to the infant. Adding to the pathogenic situation was the parents' carelessness about nudity, the mother's preoccupation with organizational activities, and the father's unpredictable rage and cruelty toward the patient. During this period, then, the patient suffered multiple traumata: his parents shifted their interest from him and concentrated their attention on his brother; his care was handed over to a domestic; he felt inferior to his father, who had the larger, more impressive organ and who was able to give the mother a baby; he felt inferior to the newborn, whom he regarded as a *wunderkind* who stole his parents' attention. Given all these circumstances, he felt worthless in the eyes of his mother and dreaded that his father would lose patience altogether and get rid of him in some manner.

He reacted to these traumata in a variety of ways. He actively wished for his father's death (e.g., he would hope that the plane would crash when his father went on business trips) but was afraid that his father would find out what was on his mind. Out of envy for the sickly infant, he contrived to break his own leg—and thus become an invalid himself—by sticking it under a trampoline while someone was jumping on it. When his brother became older, the patient teased and physically abused him only to be terrified that his brother would tell the parents. He developed his body and achieved significant athletic prowess. During his teens, however, he became paralyzed during competitions and lost to inferior opponents. There was ample analytic evidence that the activity was contaminated by fantasies of destroying his brother and father by defeating them and achieving fame. In business deals he had difficulty defending his position during negotiations because he unconsciously perceived these situations as contests with his father, a wealthy businessman.

He had difficulty in relating to women of his own social class but functioned easily with women of working class origins, whom he associated with domestics. He had a fear of getting well that derived from the traumatic withdrawal of support and the push toward independence at the time of his brother's birth. In his relationship with me, at times I was perceived as the father who he anticipated would explode with anger or tease him about his sexual life; for this reason, he tended to be apprehensive about coming to sessions after sexual adventures and he often withheld material. At times I was perceived as the mother, cold and detached; accordingly, he would become enraged and occasionally walk out of sessions if I said something that suggested that I was not understanding him.

Derivatives of this traumatic period of his life pervaded the material and disrupted his social and business relationships and activities. For him, insofar as he proceeded on the basis of this dynamic configuration, the world had a population of five: he, his parents, his brother, and the maid. The relationships among them, which were reflected in his current life, were conflict ridden and complicated.

The patient's material was characterized by frequent shifts in theme; depending on what was happening, any of the issues might appear. According to the patient's memory, an analyst he saw during his undergraduate years had focused on his patricidal fantasies; whereas the analyst who had referred him to me had stressed the idea that the patient's failure to give up his symptomatology, given his considerable insight, was attributable to the patient's fear that if he became well his parents would no longer pay attention to him. Initially, I emphasized his ambivalence toward his sibling as he struggled with academic rivalries and inhibitions in sports. In time, I offered the idea that central to the various facets of his neurosis was the loss of his mother to his father and brother at the time of the latter's birth. This idea struck him as being plausible, but yet another formulation not likely to be more helpful than the others.

In time I came to realize that I was dealing with a pathogenic residue of a traumatic period in the patient's life. I was not dealing with separate and discrete problems of self-esteem, aggression, sibling rivalry, regression, object relations, and the like, but with an organization made up of the traumatic impressions, reactive fantasies, and associated affects of the patient's fifth year. With this perspective I was able to relate his material to various facets of this period in the patient's life. Accordingly, I began to present the idea to him that his mind had two separate organizations: one that reflected his adult, realistic, adaptive personality, which was able to view situations objectively and to handle them with maturity; the other was a persistence into his adulthood of a pathogenic freeze-frame of a traumatic period in his early life. This was not a tripartite model but a bipartite model conceptually close to a mind made up of an ego and a dynamic unconscious. It was a model that implied that he was a potentially healthy person who was being disrupted by a pathogenic residue, that he did not have to gain strength from analysis, but rather that his recovery depended on his ability to give up (i.e., to recognize and work through) anachronistic patterns from childhood.

Thus, the various interpretations offered by his three analysts were all correct in that they dealt with sectors of this organization. It was not a matter of either one or another or of finding still a further problem to be uncovered. Though we continued to analyze his transference manifestations, dreams, and other derivatives as before, the understandings achieved were not regarded as ends in themselves but as manifestations of a larger and more complicated organization. With this change in perspective, the patient came to realize that his neurosis was the consequence of the disruptive effects of just such an organization. Insights now tended to fit into a dynamic scheme and to reinforce one another, whereas previously they tended to confuse him as disparate dynamic issues. As the shape and content of the warded-off residue became a partially remembered, partially inferred reality, the patient gained conviction about the analytic process.

He was able to make an increasingly clear delineation between an adaptive, observing ego (in his words, his "grown up self") and the pathogenic freeze-frame of his fifth year. His pessimism about ever achieving a normal life lifted as he found he was able to form and maintain relationships and perform sexually with women of his own social class. He handled job interviews with increasing skill and freedom from anxiety and accepted a position with a major firm in his field.

Let us return to a discussion of the two kinds of conflictual interface. According to the structural model, drives or drive derivatives arise in the id; defenses are assigned to the ego. The conflictual interface, then, resides at the interface of the ego and the id, or, in less abstract language, between the drive derivative and the defenses provided by the ego. Conceptualized in this way, there is but one conflictual interface. According to the schema model, such conflictual interfaces are encompassed by the pathogenic schema; that is, in the unmastered conflictual situations of the patient's childhood there were drive derivatives that were defended against by the immature ego; in addition, a second kind of conflictual interface was created when the disturbing conflicts were sequestered en bloc.

To return to the patient just described, during his latency he teased his brother mentally and physically. Typically he would hit him on his arms repeatedly, gradually increasing the force of his blows. He was fearful that he might hit his brother too hard and actually injure him, and he was also afraid that his brother would tell on him. In early adulthood when playing against less able opponents, he would enjoy teasing them by prolonging the action of matches, toying with them before finishing them off. His affect in these games was precisely the same as when teasing his brother. He enjoyed their frustration and pain and wished them to suffer. Eventually, both with his brother and in his sport, he developed a hysterical stiffness in his arm that prevented him from hitting his brother and playing effectively against his opponents. Anna Freud (1936) appreciated this point when she wrote of interpreting ". . . a defense mechanism, which we must attribute . . . to the ego of the same infantile period in which the id impulse first arose" (pp. 20–21). The fear of the consequences of his brother's telling on him was repeated in his fear that if he won important contests he would be out in the cold, shunned, unloved. Thus, it became clear that the match situation was perceived and processed not in terms of the patient's current reality but as a replication of his latency tormenting of his brother.

DYNAMIC SEE-SAWS

The analyst who is guided by the schema model will understand that an old scenario is being acted out. He will strive to demonstrate to the patient how the past is being repeated, sometimes in exquisite detail, with the same plot and affects, albeit the time, setting, and actors have been replaced. In other words, he will be sensitive to the interface between the adaptive, realistic ego and the pathogenic schema. If the analyst, operating with the structural model, perceives the interface as being between the patient's adult ego and the drive derivatives, then the patient is in the same situation as he was during the traumatic childhood situation. His choices, then, would be to damage his brother (defeat his opponent) and be thrown out of the family, or to accept the feeling of being an unloved, unnoticed member of the household. Each of these choices would leave the patient in an intolerably painful situation; he is trapped. Encouragement of patients in this situation must fail, save those, usually short-lived, periods when encouragement may be interpreted by the unconscious as permission. In the pathogenic schema, the greater the effort by the patient to succeed, the more intense the attempt to hurt the brother, the more intense the countervailing paralysis. A case of mental isometrics.

It is not unusual for patients over time to oscillate between untenable positions. Thus, a patient may take an aggressive attitude in dealing with an authority at work or in an academic situation only to worry that he is pushing things too far and may suffer unpleasant consequences. In response to this anxiety, he adopts a meek, conciliatory posture in the hope of appeasing the now dreaded authority and escaping some horrible retribution. In time, feeling that such self-castrating behavior is unbearable, he reacts by once again taking an aggressive attitude. Such patients frequently say that they wish they could find a middle position. Some analysts may understand such see-saw situations as instinctual conflicts between activity and passivity or between heterosexuality and homosexuality. Arlow (1963), for example, wrote:

> Where there appears to be a conflict between opposing drives, the ego takes sides with the expression of one set of drives, i.e., permits the discharge of the cathexis of one drive, in order to fend off the expression of the other, the more objectionable drive representation. Conflicts of this type . . . in actuality represent a conflict between the ego and the id, with the superego apparently in accord with the defensive position taken by the ego [p. 16].

Such a view of how the neurosis is structured is not apt to be helpful, because there is no escape. If the patient adopts a passive, submissive attitude out of fear of the consequences of his aggressiveness, one might say the ego is taking sides with the passive drive derivatives; and if the passivity becomes intolerable one might say the ego is taking sides with the aggressive drives in order to defend against the passivity. It is understandable that the patient who alternates between such polarities should seek a solution in finding some middle position.

The analyst who is guided by the schema model will view the situation differently. He will understand that the aggressive and passive fantasies and behavior and the reasons for oscillating between them are within the pathogenic schema. He will work with the patient's ego to understand what elements of this organization are being manifested in these oscillations. Thus, he may discover that as a child the patient had reacted to his father's absences with fantasies of his father's death and taking his father's position with the mother, only to become terrified when the father returned. Given this perspective, the patient will no longer be trapped into alternating between aggression and submission but will have the alternative of seeing both positions, the reason for shifting from one to the other, and the associated affects as elements of an anachronistic, pathogenic residue from the past. He will then have the newly appreciated option of striving to deal with the situation from the perspective of mature reason and judgment. This point can be illustrated by an episode which occurred early in a twice-a-week psychotherapy.

Case Illustration

It had become obvious that the patient had great difficulty with her angry feelings. Each time she criticized a family member, a fellow worker, her former therapist, or someone else, she would undo her expression of anger by pointing out the good points of the target of her aggression, rationalizing his or her behavior, or turning on herself. When we discussed this pattern of dealing with hostility, the patient revealed that she had been taught by her mother never to be angry. Her mother was a high-strung woman who reacted to stress in family life by hurling accusations, weeping, retreating to bed, and threatening to abandon the family. An older sibling was the source of much of the mother's distress, and the patient was told repeatedly that, unlike this sibling, she should be a "beam of sunshine" in the mother's life.

The patient came to her hour one afternoon angry and pessimistic about ever getting well. Her presenting symptom, a feeling that she was separated from the world by an invisible wall (see Slap, 1974), was particularly intense. She had awakened with this feeling. We reviewed the events of the previous day in an effort to understand what had exacerbated the symptom. She had been sitting at her desk, working on some project, when her supervisor walked by. As she passed the patient she paused and said to her, "We are awfully gloomy today. How about a smile?" The patient experienced a surge of rage but suppressed any expression of annoyance. She felt "out of it" for the rest of the day and went to bed early. As the patient discussed the incident, she said, "What was I to do? If I told her she was an asshole that wouldn't do me any good. I have lashed out at people before and it only got me into trouble. And if I don't express my feelings I wind up feeling terrible for days."

The patient was able to see that the supervisor's remark was identical to the sort of thing her mother used to say to her. The patient had experienced her mother's remarks for the most part with silent rage. In the current situation the patient saw only two alternatives: to express her rage or to suppress it. She was trapped with the supervisor just as she had been with her mother. Once she reacted to this current situation according to the template of her relationship with her mother, she was indeed in a no-win situation. If, on the other hand, she had perceived her supervisor's remark objectively, that is in terms of the reality of her current life, she might have made some joking rejoinder, given some simple explanation for her mood, and the incident, trivial as it was, would have been forgotten.

AFFECTS

In Chapter Three it was stressed that an important component of the sequestered schema is the affect associated with the traumata, gratifications, and fantasies of the period in which it was formed. Actually, affects, as in dream psychology, tend to be the least distorted elements of this warded-off material. Though these affects tend to be undistorted and often seem to be identical with those experiences in the past, they are often easily rationalized by the therapist as well as the patient, and so their significance for the treatment may well be overlooked.

Case Illustration

A physician who had trained and been licensed in one state opened his practice in another state. There he was involved in two incidents in which he succumbed momentarily to sexual advances from patients by embracing and kissing them. The women lodged complaints with the local medical society, and eventually he voluntarily surrendered his license. He moved back to the state where he had been licensed originally and rehabilitated himself. He entered analysis; divorced his wife, who had left him; remarried; cleared himself with the state medical board and his national specialty society; passed specialty board examinations, which he had failed in the past; and established himself in a position where he was well respected. Now, some three years after leaving his old locality in disgrace, he made preparations to attend his specialty's national meeting to be held in an exciting, cosmopolitan city in a distant part of the country. The patient became apprehensive about going to the meeting, fearing that he might run into certain old colleagues and feel disgraced.

At first glance, this might appear to be a reasonable reaction to the situation. After all, he had left his old locality under shameful circumstances, and it would not be pleasant to be reminded of a past he was trying to put behind himself. Yet this view of things was not the only possible way for him to approach the trip. For example, he might have considered that more than 12,000 physicians were expected to attend and he might not run into former colleagues; he did not even know if they would attend the meeting. And, given all that he had accomplished since leaving the old locality, he might have welcomed an opportunity to meet with these people to show them (and they might be expected to tell others) how far he had come in rehabilitating himself. Add to this the dining, museums, and other cultural attractions afforded by this city he had never visited, he might well have been more interested in the pleasures that he would experience than in how a certain few would look upon him.

The patient did not question the affect with which he anticipated the trip; it was entirely ego syntonic. When it was questioned by the analyst, the patient's thoughts and feelings about attending the convention came to be seen as derivative of an enduring traumatic situation that had arisen in the patient's childhood. His mother was a depressed, near psychotic, woman who frequently and unpredictably screamed at him. His father was a busy professional who for the most part ignored him. Belonging to an ethnic minority and being a poor athlete, he was not well accepted in school. He came to believe that there must be something very wrong about him that he should be treated this way. As an enlisted man in the service he anticipated being yelled at and was grateful when he was treated as a regular person. When he went into practice, he hated to see that there were messages on his answering machine. He was afraid that they would be complaints or notifications that he was in trouble. When others got into difficulty, he was surprised and relieved that it was not he.

This example is illustrative of treatment situations in which the affect seems appropriate to reality as it is portrayed by the patient, and yet the entire tableau is a replay of a scenario from the patient's traumatic past. The colleagues whom the patient thought he might meet were transference figures for his parents, siblings, and grade-school classmates. Attending the convention was perceived as returning home to his parents, who might unpredictably scream at him, and as returning to school, where his classmates would shun him. To say that the affect is rationalized on the basis of trouble he had gotten into with his license focuses on only a single defense against an isolated element of a complex pathogenic organization.

Although, as has been emphasized throughout, the actors and settings of the childhood situation have been substituted for in the later versions, the affects and the plot remain the same. For this reason, just as with the analysis of dreams, close attention paid to the affects may provide a clue to issues from the past that determine how current situations are experienced. Thus, a young man who enters treatment greatly depressed over having been cast aside by his girlfriend has a history of having been turned over to a succession of housemaids from early infancy on by his lawyer mother. A man raised by uncaring blue-collar parents in a squalid mill town experiences his current life as being bleak and devoid of warm relationships despite his extensive education, professional success, and the cultural and social opportunities afforded by the community where he now lives.

The affects that appear as derivatives of the past need not be simply reactions to past trauma but may arise from conflictual elements of the pathogenic organizations. This issue was addressed in a paper (Slap, 1979) about patients who complain that they are or feel like a "nothing" or a "nobody." Such feelings are readily ascribed to traumatic factors and experiences that leave an indelible impression of inferiority and inadequacy. The traumata may be related to specific phases of development. For example, an infant who is repeatedly subjected to long periods of unrelieved pain or separation anxiety is likely to feel powerless in adulthood as a result. The effect on little girls of the discovery of the anatomic difference between the sexes is pertinent here, as is the impact on the boy of the perceived differences in size, appearance, and function of the adult penis as compared with his own. Aside from such phase-related traumata, there is the effect of such factors as body defect and ridicule from parents or siblings. Such traumata may be accepted as sufficient explanation for these feelings. Yet such feelings often derive in important measure from conflicts that arise in response to the traumata of childhood; further, recognition and working through of such conflicts lead to significant therapeutic benefit, whereas failure to recognize the contribution of conflict to these affects may lead to therapeutic pessimism and stalemate.

Case Illustration

This point may be illustrated by the clinical course of a middle-aged woman who complained of feeling worthless, a nobody. She aspired to a more cultured and affluent life-style than her husband was willing to provide. Her behavior was affected, and she was prone to use malapropisms. Her husband ridiculed her pretensions. She enrolled in courses offered by a number of museums and historical societies she had joined, but failed to follow through. She attempted to become a museum guide or docent but was inhibited from doing the necessary study. She was able, however, to persuade her husband to send their only child to a fine liberal arts college away from home rather than to the local branch of the state university as her husband wished; the son went on to a prestigious professional school and subsequently became successful in his field.

The patient's father had trouble providing for the family during her childhood. When she was four, she developed rheumatic fever; she remembers her mother complaining about the fees charged by a cardiologist. She spent months in a charity hospital for children with heart disease; she regarded the experience as punishment. When the patient was five, her mother contracted tuberculosis. The patient remembered making clinic visits with her mother and sitting for long periods on a bench, waiting for her mother to be seen. The mother was hospitalized, and the patient, her father, and her older sister lived as unwelcome guests with relatives. The patient and her father shared a bed. A male cousin about her own age was the darling of the household, while she was regarded as a nuisance. After being released from the hospital, her mother played the martyr and became an active supporter of a charity hospital for chest disease.

The patient describes herself as having been a bright, vivacious girl who was unappreciated. She felt tarnished by having had to be treated in a charity hospital, by her treatment by relatives, by not being a boy, and by the sense of defect occasioned by concern over her heart. During her latency a general practitioner made a great fuss over her. His behavior became a topic of family discussion, and, whatever the substance, the patient came to believe that he wished to adopt her but that her parents refused to let her go. She had daydreams that her parents would die and that she would be adopted by this physician. During early adolescence she formed a friendship with a girl from a refined home. Rejecting her own home, she spent as much time as she could with this family.

As an adult, the patient rejected her parents, her sister, and her husband, as they reminded her of the impoverishment of the past. Her seeking culture was contaminated by fantasies of killing her parents and being adopted by the physician or by her friend's family. Guilt over these wishes ensured failure and the accompanying feeling of being a nobody, an absolutely worthless person, which reflected the opinion she held of her parents. Both the fantasies of killing the parents and the punitive nature of the nobody feeling were elements in a pathogenic organization that had arisen in her past although it seemed to her, as it did to the physician described earlier, that her failures and her low opinion of herself were based on an objective assessment of her abilities. Throughout her son's school days she had unconsciously seen him as an extension of herself; through him she would demonstrate her intellectual prowess and achieve affluence. She reacted angrily to his graduation from professional school (this is what brought her into treatment), for he had begun to assert an independent attitude. She associated this episode to the envy she had felt for her male cousin. During this period her nobody feelings were determined by guilt and punishment for impulses to castrate her son.

Analytic attention to the patient's murderous feelings toward her family members and to her self-punitive reactions to these feelings led to increased freedom to pursue her cultural interests. The affected behavior disappeared; she chaired committees and served as a docent. No longer susceptible to manipulation by her family, she was treated with more respect. She felt better about herself and no longer felt that she was a nobody.

Thus, a painful affect easily attributable to life's circumstance proved to be significantly determined by conflict contained within her sequestered schema.

Character

In the past quarter century it has been observed that the symptom neuroses described by Freud (Breuer and Freud, 1893–95), and typical of the early history of psychoanalysis, have become significantly less frequently seen; they have been replaced by character pathology. To put the matter differently, the fantasies that underlie the pathology find expression in the manner in which the person relates to his important objects and to society in general. In current terminology, the more extreme forms of character pathology are called personality disorders. Thus we have such entities as paranoid, dependent, histrionic, narcissistic, and schizoid personalities. The DSM-III (American Psychiatric Association, 1980) description of most of the subtypes begins with the passage: "The following [symptoms] are characteristic of the individual's current and long term functioning, are not limited to episodes of illness, and cause either significant impairment in social or occupational functioning or subjective distress" (p. 315).

Case Illustration

We shall take up a case whose features entailed many of the attributes of the histrionic personality as described in the DSM-III and who would be properly diagnosed as a histrionic personality. It will become clear that the histrionic qualities manifested by the patient were derived from a fantasy in which she was seeking the idealized, glamorized father who had deserted his family on the Christmas eve of her sixth year.

The patient's family lived in a lower-class section of a seashore resort city. Her father drove a jitney; her mother was a housewife. The patient had an older and a younger sister. When the father disappeared, the patient resisted sharing the bitterness felt toward him by her mother and other relatives. Instead she idealized him. There was a rumor that he had gone to California, and she had the fantasy that he had struck it rich and that someday they would be happily reunited. At the same time, she denigrated her depressed, self-pitying mother. The mother supported the family by taking several regular lovers, "uncles" to the children. The patient recalled that one of these "uncles" would call on the mother early in the day. The patient would be given money to take her little sister to an amusement park and entertain her. When riding the carousel, the patient would select a mother and father from the many watching their children and imagine that they were her own parents; she would wave and blow kisses in their direction. As she grew older, she accepted babysitting jobs in a more affluent section of the city. She would find family picture albums and look through them, imagining that she was a member of the family for whom she was sitting.

She majored in art at a state-supported university while carrying on numerous affairs with dental students at an Ivy League institution. She tended to glamorize these young men while acquiring the reputation among them of being a whore. In time, she ran out of funds and was desperate when she was rescued by a depressed young man who taught art in the public school. He was quite needy and believed that she would be forever grateful to him for having rescued her from starvation; he married her.

At the core of her pathology was a schema organized around the traumatic loss of her father when she was five years old. Reacting to this loss with splitting, she idealized the father and debased the mother who managed to raise her three children under most difficult circumstances. Accordingly, the patient sought to escape from her poor, depressed home and find a glamorous, affluent life, which she associated with her father, who, in her fantasy, was living in California or some other exotic distant place. She perceived and reacted to her husband as the depressed, impoverished mother. Soon they had children, and the patient experienced her life as a replication of her childhood situation. Seeking to escape, she had numerous casual affairs, frequently with men from distant shores who struck her as glamorous, for example, a seaman off an Israeli freighter.

One Friday she used her hour to extol the virtues of the mixed neighborhood in which she lived. There were black and white, rich and poor, professionals and blue-collar workers. Over the weekend she had attended , without her husband, a posh benefit for an art foundation. There she met two wealthy young men who were rapturous over living in Princeton; they told her of the beauty, the intellectual climate, the celebrity of many of its residents. When she came to her next session, she was filled with unrealistic plans to persuade her husband, whose job required that he live in Philadelphia, to sell their home in what she now characterized as a marginal neighborhood and to use the proceeds for a down payment on a home in Princeton.

This vignette illustrates how shallow were her convictions and the ease with which she idealized and debased given situations, sometimes the same situations. Her affect and manner were distinctly histrionic, as were often her makeup and dress. She was reminiscent of a series of magazine advertisements that portrayed flamboyant costume drama scenes, for example, a voluptuous, scantily clad young woman captured by a band of pirates. The headline would read "Who is Ron Rico?" implying that he was a romantic actor in the tradition of Valentino. The printed material below the picture revealed that Ron Rico was a brand of Puerto Rican rum. The patient was familiar with this series of advertisements, and it became a useful device in treatment, helping her become aware of her histrionic character.

A turning point in the treatment occurred when, in anticipation of attending the city's Beaux Arts ball, she mentioned that she had from time to time stolen clothing from an exclusive department store. She rationalized that since she was poor and the clientele of the store wealthy, the expense of her pilferage would be divided among many people who could easily afford the few pennies it would cost them. Therefore, she asked, wouldn't I agree that taking merchandise from this store was not really stealing? I replied that, since by any definition what she was contemplating was stealing and would be so regarded by the store, I could not agree. She became furious with me and for a few weeks debated whether or not to continue the treatment. I had become valuable to her since I seemed to understand her better than had her prior therapists, and she had idealized me; in the transference I was in the category of the wonderful stranger/father whom she would someday meet and be rescued by. Now, although enraged with me, she was reluctant to get rid of me, which would be more in keeping with her usual use of splitting. She could no longer regard me as all good, but I was too valuable to toss away as all bad. She stayed with the therapy and emerged from this episode a more sober, insightful, and sophisticated person. Ultimately, after her husband died, she settled into an enduring, mutually gratifying relationship with a Scandinavian physicist whom she had initially stereotypically idealized as an exotic foreigner.

Thus we see that the patient dealt with the traumatic loss of the father with the fantasy that some day she would be united with this idealized figure while denying his failed obligations to his wife and children; at the same time she denigrated her mother as a bad, ungratifying object. Derivatives of this configuration appeared in her indulgence in fantasies about having other parents and families and later in the transference and in liaisons with Ivy League students, an Israeli seaman, and others perceived as glamorous and wealthy. They were manifest too in her wish to move to Princeton. The ease with which she formed and acted out these fantasies gave her character a histrionic stamp.

According to the schema model, the painful impressions and situations of childhood that are not mastered and absorbed by the immature mind become the nidus for the formation of a separate mental organization, the sequestered schema. The sequestered schema may be viewed as a freeze-frame of the painful period of its formation and encompasses traumatic impressions and situations, reactive fantasies, associated affects, object relationships, and cognitive functioning. Insofar as this organization is active, it perceives and processes current relationships and events according to the template established in early life and not in keeping with a mature and objective perceptual capacity. Once again, in Piagetian terms, assimilation prevails over accommodation.

The clinical material described in this chapter has been presented with the aim of demonstrating that the psychopathology of patients in psychoanalysis and psychoanalytically oriented psychotherapy arises as a consequence of the activity of these organizations. In each of the cases, the patient's symptomatology was related to configurations arising from the traumata of childhood. We have attempted to show how this replication applies to, among the various aspects of the material, affects, character, inhibitions and defenses. In the next chapter, we shall show how this model applies to dreaming, transference, working through, and other psychoanalytic concepts.

CHAPTER FIVE

◄ ►

Dreaming, Transference, Working Through, and Other Psychoanalytic Concepts

The schema model, we have asserted, is internally consistent. There are no internal contradictions in the conceptualization of its component elements. Further, psychoanalytic concepts, some of which have an uncertain relationship to the structural model, are easily accommodated by the schema model. For example, repetitive phenomena are not attributed to a reified *repetition compulsion* but are understood as reflecting the activity over time of the pathogenic sequestered schema. The relation of trauma to the model has been explored in earlier chapters. These concepts are logical and inevitable corollaries of the schema model.

In this chapter we shall try to show that the interpretation of dreams is entirely consistent with the schema model and conversely that the schema model lends an internally consistent theoretical basis for dealing with dreams. We understand the dream as the product of the interaction of the sequestered schema with a current day event or situation. The sequestered schema is understood as an organization of the mind, having at its core traumatic impressions and situations of the past, which has been separated from the generally interconnected mass of ideas and which functions at a primitive cognitive level in which assimilation prevails over accommodation. The sequestered schema encompasses in its organization, along with the traumatic issues, the reactive fantasies and associated affects of the traumatic period, the later relevant painful and gratifying events that have been assimilated into its organization. Thus, as we understand dreams, some circumstance of the dream day has been perceived as being pertinent to the sequestered schema, which has reacted to this perception in terms of its anachronistic template. Thus, the new perception is being connected to (assimilated by) the old organization. This understanding is entirely compatible with the work of Hartmann (1973), a psychoanalytically informed dream researcher:

> It is reasonable that a new piece of input from waking life is often connected with an old brain pathway to which it is in some way related. (Or, in psychoanalytic terms, a manifest dream element derives from a day residue plus an old wish or fear it has "aroused.") More generally, primary process in dreaming—primitive connections, large discharges of energy, opposites occurring together—can all be seen as characteristic of a "reconnecting" process in which daytime residues are reconnected to large, old, and thus "primitive" pathways or brain storage systems. . . .
>
> Thus the overall hypothesis I am proposing is that during D-sleep [dream or REM sleep] new connections are formed, especially in cortical areas served by ascending catecholamine pathways, and that specifically new connections are formed between daytime memories that have somehow been left unconnected and old pathways. This is entirely compatible with Freud's formulation that dreams are made up of day residue material and old wishes. However, I would add that it need not necessarily be *wishes*, although certainly old wishes and fears may be among the primary and most primitive channels for forming connections, and during dreams daytime material is connected to these old systems or channels [pp. 133–34].

There are two implications of this passage worth our attention. First, when one considers the myriad impressions, activities, and interactions with others that a person experiences or performs during a day, we realize how selective the dream process is, that is, how the latent dream thoughts are concerned with only a certain kind of material. They deal with painful and conflictual matters. Even where dreams seem to be purely expressions of wishes, they arise from situations of deprivation, as when the starving explorer dreams of a sumptuous feast. Might the circumstance that dreams at their root deal with painful and conflictual matters be explained by the consideration that dreams involve the connection of new material with a part of the mind that has special cognitive properties, namely, the sequestered schema? Hartmann does refer to the integration of new material with special parts of the mind: "large, old, and thus 'primitive' pathways or brain storage systems" (p. 133). The integration of new experience with the generally interconnected main mass of ideas, the ego, would not seem to require the dream process.

The second implication is the status of the wish fulfillment theory of dreaming. Hartmann writes that the concept that during D-sleep connections are made between daytime memories and old pathways is compatible with Freud's formulation that dreams are made up of day residue material and old wishes. Hartmann hastens to add, however, "that it need not necessarily be *wishes*" (p. 133). In their consideration of the relationship of dreams to the structural theory, Arlow and Brenner (1964) wrote as follows:

> We try today to understand the patient's inner *conflicts*, not merely the infantile *wishes* which comprise the instinctual aspect of those conflicts. We try to make clear to each patient both the anti-instinctual and the instinctual aspects of his conflicts and to trace the history of both back to the experiences and events of childhood which were decisively important in determining the original nature of his conflicts, their subsequent course, and their influence on the various aspects of his mental development [p. 141].

Although Arlow and Brenner were writing in support of a model that we feel is flawed, this statement of their understanding of dreams and approach to dream interpretation is compatible with the schema model. It understands infantile wishes as but one component in a larger organization and encompasses "the experiences and events of childhood which were decisively important" in the patient's neurosis. In this connection we are reminded of a mot attributed to Otto Isakower to the effect that in dream interpretation "we no longer go on wish hunts."

Freud was driven to acknowledge exceptions to the wish fulfillment theory of dreams. He recognized that unpleasurable dreams may be dreams of punishment. On one hand, he attempted to explain away this apparent exception by asserting that the dreamer wished that he "may be punished for a repressed and forbidden wishful impulse" (Freud, 1900, pp. 557–558). He acknowledged, however, that in punishment dreams, the dream-constructing wish belongs not to the repressed but to the ego. "Thus, punishment-dreams indicate the possibility that the ego may have a greater share than was supposed in the construction of dreams," he wrote. He developed this theme more fully later (Freud, 1925b) and in 1933 implicated the superego. In this way, consistent with Arlow and Brenner's (1964) explication, Freud acknowledged that the latent dream thoughts might draw from any of the macrostructures in their formation. Freud also recognized that an exception to the wish fulfillment theory of dreams was the type of dream in which traumata were repeated. These included such traumata of adult life as occur in combat or in railway accidents and also dreams "which bring to memory the psychical traumas of childhood" (Freud, 1920, p. 32). He posited that the original function of the dream may not have been wish fulfillment, but the binding of traumata.

The following presentation of a case that came to a successful conclusion with the analysis of a dream that filled in the missing details of a traumatic event that lay at the core of the patient's neurosis illustrates our understanding of the dream process according to the schema model. Examples of dreams from earlier in her analysis will be shown to deal with circumscribed sectors of the patient's pathogenic sequestered schema.

The patient insisted that her analysis could never be satisfactorily terminated unless the details of a particular traumatic occurrence of her childhood were uncovered. A dream occurring during the ninth year of her analysis led to the reconstruction of a primal scene event that organized a number of elements previously recalled and was entirely convincing to both the patient and me. A residual symptom, a sensation that her gums were swelling and her teeth falling out, which occurred whenever she entered my office, abruptly disappeared. She now felt that there was no reason to continue in analysis, and we ended the treatment approximately two months after this dream was reported.

Elsewhere (Slap, 1982), I have reported a fragment of understanding achieved about her then incompletely reconstructed primal scene experience. This experience occurred soon after the patient's fourth birthday, when her mother was in the ninth month of pregnancy with the patient's only sibling, a sister.

> Dreams, associations, and transference phenomena—along with her dim memory of the event—suggested that her mother refused to have intercourse with the father out of a fear of harming the baby and that the patient's parents had performed "sixty-nine" instead [p. 428].

A parapraxis indicated that the patient had interpreted her father's mouthing of her mother's genitals as biting off the penis of the unborn baby.

From time to time the patient would awaken with anxiety in the middle of the night and find that the time was 3:45. The patient attributed this repeated occurrence to the primal scene experience in the following way: There was a large clock hanging outside a jewelry store easily visible through the bedroom window to the patient in her crib. The patient remembered vividly that the clock read 3:45 at the time of the experience; that is, a screen memory in which her attention had been defensively focused on a detail outside the room in an attempt to avoid what was going on inside the room. As the patient continued to work on recovering this experience, it came to her that her father had struck her in the face sometime during the event and had angrily told the mother that "she [the patient] shouldn't be in here anyway." The patient had no idea what had provoked this anger.

One day the patient reported the following event:

> I woke precisely at 3:45—it was disgusting—with a dream. Maybe it was stimulated by a sports broadcast. We

> [husband and patient] had seen a football game at the Spectrum. We left before the last few minutes of play to get out before the hordes descended. We were driving west. Suddenly Ed [husband] jammed on the brakes. He made a U-turn back into the parking lot. There were no cars there. It was empty. He started to drive down a ramp into the bowels of the building. There was a crowd of people there. They were short. I did not want to hurt them. I shouted, "Don't!" Ed turned to me and his face was a death's head with his teeth barely hanging on by a thread. . . .

The patient connected the 3:45 awakening to the primal scene experience. Her remark that "it was disgusting" was intended as a commentary on the repetitiousness of such awakenings, although it seemed plausible to us both that the adjective alluded to the experience itself. She associated the changes in direction from west to east and from the upper part of the building to the lower to the "sixty-nine" position we had reconstructed earlier. While this seemed valid as far as it went, it seemed that these changes in direction reflected a shift in position from "sixty-nine" to genital intercourse. The patient's traveling with the male aggressor (husband, father) implied that she had identified with the male during the primal scene experience, which was in keeping with her phallic orientation. It appeared that the father had interrupted the "sixty-nine" intercourse when he was approaching a climax—"we left before the last few minutes of play to get out before the hordes descended" and then turned to the mother's genital—"parking lot." Evidently as he was about to enter—"he started to drive down a ramp into the bowels of the building"—the patient became afraid that the child or children within the mother's claustrum—"crowd of people, they were short"—would be injured and cried out "Don't." The father then turned toward her, having lost his erection—"his face was a death's head with the teeth barely hanging on by a thread." That her crying out had caused him to lose his erection accounted for his becoming so angry as to smack her and to complain to the mother that she should not have been there. The patient had some recollection of being taken into the bathroom and having her mouth, which had begun to bleed as a result of the blow, washed by her mother. This blow to the mouth and her symbolic use of "teeth barely hanging on by a thread" appeared to be additional determinants for her fantasies of having her teeth fall out.

During a period of eight days of the patient's third year of analysis, she reported three dreams experienced at sleep onset (Slap, 1977). The first was understood as being expressive of her sense of defect in not having a penis and her reactive wish to obtain one. Important events from the patient's third year were being recalled or convincingly reconstructed. One of these events was a visit to a doctor that was prompted by her parents' concern that she was not talking; she had been slow to walk as well. The doctor said that she might not develop normally: "You never can tell with preemies." The patient recalled sitting in an armchair, very upset after this visit. A housemaid defended her to her mother, saying, "It is not the poor girl's fault." The maid was dismissed soon thereafter. The patient had the idea that she had been punished by her father or her mother for not having developed normally. It may have been at this time that her father had screamed at her, "Stupid! Stupid! Stupid!" She was very disappointed about her inability to remember the details of the punishment. I remarked that it was characteristic of her to complain that she was not a capable analysand, although she was actually quite adept. That night, as she was falling asleep, she dreamed the following:

> I was a little girl sitting in an armchair, thumbing through a catalogue. It was black and white, indistinct, overinked and blurred. My mother came up from behind me and startled me. She said, "Why not leave well enough alone?" I saw her disappear around a corner.

Associating to the dream, the patient recalled looking in the newspaper for the review of a show she had seen the night before (the review was not there) and watching a late night talk show on which the host read letters children had written to a department store Santa Claus; one boy had listed the items he wanted from a catalogue.

The interpretation mutually arrived at was that the patient, who identified with the boy, wanted something, a phallus, but was told by her mother to resign herself to not having it, to leave well enough alone. The black and white catalogue in the dream referred both to the newspaper from which the review was missing and to the catalogue mentioned in the television program. It also referred to her mother's genital, the connection being black public hair in contrast with white skin.[1] The blurred, indistinct character of the catalogue seemed to represent a defense against the horrifying sight of her mother's genital during a primal scene experience, to which she was alluding in her mention of the show and the television program.

The mother's statement in the dream was in part derived from the previous analytic hour. When the patient had expressed annoyance over the gap in her memory, I had told her in effect that she was doing well enough as it was. One element of the manifest content of the dream was acted out during the hour in which she reported the dream: she had been startled and claimed that my voice had suddenly become louder as I shifted in my chair.

The second and third dreams were traumatic dreams deriving from the primal scene experience. The second dream went as follows:

> Two coffins, one containing a king dressed in black lamé, the other a queen (who looked like my mother) dressed in white lamé and wearing a wimple, were orbiting wildly about one another, but not touching. They were dead. There was also a tiny coffin with a baby in it. The baby was asleep, not dead. The baby was wearing a locket with a cameo my mother has on its cover. The baby was swaddled around with white, pink, gauzy material. I was afraid the larger coffins would hit the baby's coffin. Somehow, at the same time I was preoccupied with the plural of beef . . . beeves, dwarf . . . dwarves.

[1]Tarachow (1961) reported two cases in which interest in color contrast was found to be derived from the contrast between white abdominal skin and female pubic hair. The dream symbol of black and white appeared in several of my patient's previous dreams and was understood to have had that meaning.

No day residue was found for the second dream, save for the analytic hour during which the first dream had been considered and the issue of her having witnessed her parents in the sexual act had been discussed. The lamé apparel of the figures in the coffins was found to refer to the costume of the corps de ballet of the show she had seen two nights before. The opening number, a "stunner" according to the patient, had the women dressed as witches in black lamé with long lengths of cloth streaming from their hats. The baby, she felt, referred to herself, asleep; in hindsight, it was more likely the sister. The locket reminded her of the locket held by the blind girl in the classic film about two women trying to survive during the French Revolution, *Orphans of the Storm*. Since coffins had often appeared in her dreams and this dream seemed to derive from a traumatic primal scene experience, I started to ask if her parents' bed could in any way be likened to a coffin. The patient interrupted my sentence to volunteer that her parents' bed was a gloomy, Empire affair with a large, squarish footboard and headboard. The sideboards were prominent as well and the bed did look like a coffin. The top of the footboard and the headboard were curled in such a way as to remind her of coffin handles.

The patient remembered that many years before, she had come upon the word *beeves* in something she was reading and was puzzled by it. When she looked in the dictionary and found that it was the plural of beef, she felt "so stupid." The idea of a dwarf seemed to relate to deficiencies, especially her failure to talk and her "stupidity"; to the blind girl; her mother's genital; and other details from this period of treatment.

Six nights later, the patient had another hypnogogic experience:

> As I was dozing off, that photograph of the girl kneeling over the student who was shot at Kent State, screaming, her arms outstretched, came very strongly into my mind. In this image she was kneeling beside a closed coffin: I have no idea who was inside. While in the Kent State photograph the prominent thing was the outstretched arms, in my image it was the gaping, oval mouth. The girl was screaming a silent scream. The image was very vivid and

> real. I couldn't get it out of my mind and I turned over to get rid of it.

The "vivid and real" quality of the third dream indicates that it is expressive of a real event. The patient felt that the silent, screaming girl was herself watching her parents' sexual activity and that the gaping, oval mouth represented a mental image of her mother's genital. The photograph in reality portrayed a young woman screaming in horror over the body of a male student who had been shot by a National Guardsman; in the light of the clarifying dream that ended the analysis, the person in the closed coffin was her sister.

Later in her analysis, at a time when the patient was struggling with castrating impulses in the transference, she reported a dream in which she was mocked by me. It became clear that this was a punishment dream in which I mocked her in retaliation for her silent ridicule of me the previous day. On that day, as the session preceding hers was ending, a building employee knocked on my office door to inform me of a bomb scare; there had been a telephone message saying that a bomb would go off in the building in a half hour. The preceding analysand left. I had a short discussion with the patient in the doorway between the waiting room and the consultation room, and we decided, although neither of us took the threat seriously, to cancel the hour. Before she left, I took a moment to get her bill for the previous month from my desk and handed it to her. The following day the patient reported a dream:

> You were standing in the doorway of your office. You were very tall, taller than you actually are. You were mocking me with your head tilted to one side, your mouth open, your tongue hanging out of the corner of your mouth.

The patient associated my standing in the doorway to our conversation the previous day. She had been amused by my handing her the bill under the circumstances and had had the satirical thought: the goddamn building is about to go up in smoke and all he can think about is his bill. In the dream I was extremely tall, filling the doorway—a phallus. At the same time, I was showing her what she was by mocking her. My head cocked to the side with my tongue askew and drooping represented her castrated condition.

The pathogenic schema that lay at the root of the patient's neurosis may be summarized as follows: The patient as a little girl had believed that her lack of a penis was attributable to an injury she had suffered in utero as a consequence of her parents' sexual activity. There was evidence that she had fantasies that this injury had occurred as a result of cunnilingus and also phallic penetration. A particularly traumatic sequence of events occurred when she, at the age of four years, witnessed her parents' lovemaking and cried out when she believed the fetus the mother was carrying was about to be injured by the father's phallus. Her crying out interrupted the lovemaking and caused the father to lose his erection. Furious at the interruption, he rushed to his daughter's crib and struck her in the mouth.

Her dreams during the course of the analysis were reflective of the manifold facets of her pathogenic schema. In the material just presented, one dream deals with her disappointment in not having a penis; in another we see her vindictive wish to castrate her father and her punishment for this wish; and in others we see partial replication of the traumatic primal scene, which included these and other elements of this time in her life and which lay at the core of her neurosis.

Transference

The first use of the concept of transference in the psychoanalytic sense appears in Breuer and Freud (1905). Freud wrote:

> . . . the patient is frightened at finding that she is transferring on to the figure of the physician the distressing ideas which arise from the content of the analysis. This is frequent, and indeed in some analyses a regular, occurrence. Transference on to the physician takes place through a *false connection* [p. 301].

In this usage, ideas from within the psychic contents are transferred or carried over onto the therapist; accordingly, transference has been described as a displacement or projection of feelings about the important figures of the patient's childhood onto the therapist. The schema model conceives of transference as having a different, in a way, opposite, meaning. According to the schema model, the phenomenology ascribed to the transference is brought about by misperception; that is, the sequestered schema perceives the analyst in a manner determined by an old and anachronistic template. Thus, transference requires no special explanation or mechanisms. Understood in this way, many of the debates about intra- and extra-analytic transferences and the centrality of the transference neurosis become moot. The activity of the pathogenic schema involves the person of the therapist with varying intensity and varying consistency of the role in which the therapist is cast. These variations appear to result from many factors, including the severity of the illness and the nature of the fantasy system, on one hand, and the age, gender, personality, and behavior of the analyst, on the other.

Wachtel (1980) wrote of the relevance of the Piagetian concepts of schema and assimilation to the phenomenology of transference:

> Transference reactions, in Piaget's terms, may be seen simply as reflecting schemas which are characterized by a strong predominance of assimilation over accommodation. The experience with the analyst is assimilated to schemas shaped by earlier experiences, and there is very little accommodation to the actualities of the present situation which make it different from the former experience [p. 63].

and:

> Transference . . . can be understood as the result of a state of affairs in which assimilation is strongly predominant. . . . Since assimilation is strongly predominant, it does not take a particularly close fit to activate the transference schema. So two very different analysts may, in

> separate analyses with the same patient, be subjectively experienced in very similar fashion by the patient. The schema is easy to activate, and it does not change very readily despite the lack of fit [p. 64].

Though Wachtel focuses on the role of assimilation in transference, assimilation has a much broader scope. As a result of the assimilation activity of the pathogenic schema, the neurotic selectively distorts his perception of his entire world. Paradigmatic of psychoanalysis as a therapy is, of course, the use of transference reactions to reconstruct from its derivatives the infantile neurosis. The distortions that occur in analysis reflect the process of the patient's pathogenic schema assimilating the representation of the analyst to it. Transference interpretations attempt to reduce the assimilative process regarding the analyst; these and other interpretations ultimately reconstruct for the patient his pathogenic sequestered schema and its influence in his life.

Working Through

We conceive of working through as follows: The ego, having repressed the pathogenic schema, continues to avoid, insofar as it can, any recognition of its content. The motivation for this continued shunning of the repressed schema is the avoidance of anxiety, shame, and other painful affects. Demonstrating to the patient the repeated motifs, themes, and other derivatives of the repressed schema brings about a new ability for self-observation and an understanding of the anachronistic nature of the disturbing fantasies. As a consequence, there is a shift in attitude to the repressed schema, which the ego now strives to know and explore. When a given derivative is analyzed, the ego—a schema in its own right—assimilates the derivative. That is, it understands the derivative in terms of what it really is: a manifestation of an anachronistic fantasy. Many repeated analyses of derivatives give the ego confidence in the analytic process and added ability to recognize and understand further derivatives. Over the course of time in successful treatments the ego develops increasing mastery, and the sequestered schema loses power and influence.

The ability to sublimate grows as the patient's life activities are purged of their assimilated conflictual element through progressive accommodation to reality. Perception becomes less selective, and the patient can consider all the available data, rather than being restricted by the anxiety associated with certain objects, events, and activities by virtue of their being assimilated by the repressed schema. In addition to the working through of pathogenic schemata through interpretation, a second significant accommodative process occurs in treatment, namely, the patient's identifications with the therapist. In general, early in treatment, the therapist is assimilated as a prototypical figure from childhood within the repressed schema. Later, the patient's ego expands as a consequence of accommodation to, or identification with, the therapist's cognitive style and reality orientation. Finally, the schema concept suggests a new look at criteria for termination of treatment. The unconscious, understood as a repressed schema, loses some of its mystery and appearance of boundlessness; it seems more finite and susceptible to mastery. Consequently, the clinician might take into account the degree of reconstruction of the definable repressed schema as well as the extent to which its power has been eroded and the ego concomitantly expanded.

Implications for the Theory of Defenses

In the proposed model, the repressed unconscious is understood to be a sequestered schema that contains impulses, fantasies, traumatic impressions, defenses, affective dispositions, and so forth. From the genetic vantage, we conceive that in childhood a conflictual situation arose that evoked defensive efforts on a more or less ad hoc basis—identification, reaction formation, regression, and the like were employed in response to specific incidents provoking instinctual temptations, disappointments, and danger situations. As the conflicts became more organized and less susceptible to alleviation by environmental gratifications, a new defense appeared, namely, sequestering or repression. Repression, unlike the others indicated earlier, did not operate on an ad hoc basis, but constituted an effort to put aside the entire organized conflictual complex; in repression, to use Freud's terminology, a part of the ego was pushed into the id as the repressed unconscious. When this disruption of the normal interconnectedness of the unitary schema occurs, resulting in a cleavage between the ego and the warded off or sequestered material, not only are temptations, fantasies, affective dispositions, and traumatic impressions involved, but the earlier defensive strivings are included as well.

In the adult neuroses, we observe the *return of the repressed*, which in terms of the proposed model would be understood as a failure of the effort to continue walling off the previously sequestered schema; with this failure, the various components of the latter achieve freer access to consciousness and play a greater role in the mentation and behavior of the patient. While all thought and action are multiply determined, with the breakdown of repression the influence of the previously sequestered, pathogenic schema will become greater.

Because Freud (1937) assigned defense to one system, the ego, and the warded-off drive derivatives to another, the id, he had to deal with the troublesome issue of unconscious defenses by declaring that part of the ego both was unconscious and had to be defended against by the ego itself. Thus, there are two layers of conflictual interfaces. The ego struggles with the unconscious ego which in turn defends against the id material.

> The therapeutic effect depends on making conscious what is repressed, in the widest sense of the word, in the id. We prepare the way for this making conscious by interpretations and constructions, but we have interpreted only for ourselves not for the patient so long as the ego holds on to its earlier defenses and does not give up its resistances. Now these resistances, although they belong to the ego, are nevertheless unconscious and in some sense separated off within the ego. . . . One might suppose that it would be sufficient to treat them like portions of the id and, by making them conscious, bring them into connection with the rest of the ego. In this way, we should

> suppose, one half of the task of analysis would be accomplished; we should not reckon on meeting with a resistance against the uncovering of resistances [pp. 238–239].

This view of the relationship of the defenses to his model of the mind did not stand Freud in good stead in the conduct of his analyses. He found that

> during the work on the resistances the ego withdraws . . . from the agreement on which the analytic situation is founded. The ego ceases to support our efforts at uncovering the id; it opposes them, disobeys the fundamental rule of analysis, and allows no further derivatives of the repressed to emerge. We cannot expect the patient to have a strong conviction of the curative power of analysis [p. 239].

He saw the difficulties presented by these resistances as a limiting factor in the successful outcome of analyses and expressed this assessment in a pessimistically toned passage:

> The effect brought about in the ego by the defenses can rightly be described as an "alteration of the ego" if by that we understand a deviation from the fiction of a normal ego which would guarantee unshakable loyalty to the work of analysis. It is easy, then, to accept the fact, shown by daily experience, that the outcome of an analytic treatment depends essentially on the strength and on the depth of root of these resistances that bring about an alteration in the ego. Once again we are confronted with the importance of the quantitative factor, and once again we are reminded that analysis can only draw upon definite and limited amounts of energy which have to be measured against the hostile forces. And it seems as if victory is in fact as a rule on the side of the big battalions [pp. 239–240].

Here, then, is a clear distinction between the structural and schema models. According to the former, the original defenses employed against the drive derivatives are assigned to the same system as the adult ego. According to the proposed model, such defenses are components of the pathogenic schema and are indicative of defenses employed at the time of the original traumatic situation and of defensive activity that occurred as part of later events and situations assimilated by the pathogenic schema. My experience in using this model in both conducting and supervising analyses does not confirm Freud's finding that these defenses are obstacles that as a rule defeat the therapeutic efficacy of psychoanalysis.

The breakdown of repression is more complete in borderline and other severe disorders, which give rise to an even stronger and clearer emergence of the previously sequestered, pathogenic schemas and to regression to earlier precursors of repression, such as projection and some forms of splitting. Ultimately, in psychosis, reality may be dealt with in a completely assimilative manner, leading to its distortion or replacement by fantasy derived from the pathological schema. Thus, in this view, *the return of the repressed* is actually the manifestation of the activity of assimilation of the schema, which becomes more apparent as repression breaks down.

The sequestering we speak of is not a theoretical concept but an event that often takes place under the eye of the clinician. It is common in child analysis to see children who are disturbed by conflicts precipitated by a maturational spurt or by such events as the separation of parents or the birth of a sibling. In these cases, the analyst feels he is seeing neurosis in *statu nascendi*. With prompt treatment, such cases often yield easily to treatment. If untreated, the conflicts become organized and are said to be "internalized"; they often become much more difficult, or, in some cases, impossible, to treat successfully. This "internalization of the conflict" is precisely what we refer to by the term "sequestering."

Lines of Development

Anna Freud's (1965) concept of developmental lines is consistent with Piaget's account of schema development. She gave as a prototype for developmental lines the sequence of stages involved in the transition from dependency to emotional self-reliance and adult object relations. Additional examples ranged from sucking to rational eating, from wetting and soiling to bladder and bowel control, from the body to the toy, and from play to work. For the most part the steps along a particular developmental line were identified without examination of the nature of the continuity between these selected points in the sequence. Yet she did allude to this continuity succinctly:

> Whatever level has been reached by any given child in any of these respects represents the results of interaction between drive and ego-superego development and their reaction to environmental influences, i.e., between maturation, adaptation, and structuralization. Far from being theoretical abstractions, developmental lines, in the sense here used, are historical realities which, when assembled, convey a convincing picture of an individual child's personal achievements or, on the other hand, of his failures in personality development [p. 64].

As there is progress along the lines of development, the levels achieved by the child are succeeded by more advanced levels. The impetus for change comes from somatic maturation and environmental influence; the structures involved change as a consequence of interaction with these stimuli. Though the terminology differs, the conceptual understanding of the nature of the growth and continuity of the developmental lines is identical with schema formation: a repetitive pattern (schema) is established: new stimuli impinge on the schema (assimilation); the schema adapts (accommodates) to the new stimuli; and a change in the schema results. This ongoing process determines progress along developmental lines or, in Piagetian terms, in schema development.

CHAPTER SIX

◄ ►

Treatment

If a model of the mind is to have clinical utility, it should portray pathology in a manner consistent with what is encountered in our consulting rooms. This model should inform and guide the therapeutic efforts of practitioners to help their patients gain the insight and self-awareness that will lead to partial or complete resolution and consequent diminution of symptomatology and suffering. These remarks apply to all insight-oriented therapies, whether they be psychoanalysis or psychoanalytically oriented therapies. Accordingly, we make no sharp distinctions between psychoanalysis and psychoanalytically oriented psychotherapy, and we are in sympathy with Wallerstein (1989), who concluded that "though the differences between psychoanalysis and expressive psychotherapy . . . are there and real, the boundaries and the seemingly specific deployments are . . . much less clear-cut . . . (p. 20)." Not only is it hard to specify the theoretical differences but, confirming what is commonly known, Wallerstein indicated that when psychoanalysts discuss informally what they actually do the blurring of modalities appears to be far more widespread than one would expect from presentations at official settings.

Let us return to the lawyer described in Chapter Four. At the age of a year and a half he had suffered a traumatic separation from his mother, and this injury was compounded after her recovery when she became pregnant and delivered a second son. His father was a professional who worked with the federal government in a position that was perceived as providing widespread benefits to the nation. The patient, as he had done before, had made a career change some months prior to the period we are looking at. In this instance, as in the past, he had been courted by the head of an organization whose activities had the potential to help mankind. Once on board, however, he encountered problems that led him to be concerned about the prospects for his new affiliation and the wisdom of his move. Meanwhile, his closest friend, a man slightly younger than he who had followed him in his training, was prospering. The patient wondered if he were squandering his talents in a worthless enterprise. During this period, the patient became increasingly angry with his wife; he felt that she was depriving him of love. Uncharacteristically, he behaved harshly with his young sons. He felt that life was unfair. He was depressed and bitter. He tried to defend against his hostile impulses by being sweet and understanding, but he would often lose control and have temper tantrums at home and at work.

At this juncture, the patient's life, viewed from the outside, was not at all bad. There were, it was true, some problems with his business and marriage (the latter largely of his own making); still, these problems were certainly manageable. He was financially secure and could easily find employment in the event the organization failed. He and his family were in excellent health. Yet, from a subjective point of view, it was clear, the patient was experiencing his life as he had during the period surrounding the birth of his younger brother.

His sense of being unloved by his mother was replicated affectively in his relationship with his wife. His friend's financial success stimulated his old feelings that the new baby would outshine him, and his rage at this sibling was reflected in his behavior toward his own children. His awe of his father's place in the family and his professional accomplishments, along with the fear that the new baby would turn out to be a *wunderkind*, led to a desperate striving to emulate his father. This need to defend against his feelings of insignificance contributed to the several career changes, each made with the belief that he had found the ticket to greatness. His current life was a freeze-frame of his fourth year.

Although there is actually no mainstream consensus about what the structural model entails, it seems fair to say that according to the structural model demands are made on the ego by the drives, the superego, and the external world. Usually, discussion centers on the ego's struggle with drive derivatives, and at times the ego is depicted as acting at the behest of the superego.

In the patient just described, we see that his ego had to contend with a variety of drive derivatives. There were his attachment to his mother and his hatred of her for betraying him by having his baby brother; there was the need to defend against wishes to murder his brother and to surpass his father. Because he felt weak and inadequate, he sought mentors who would enable him to attain strength and power; this tendency to seek out mentors was derived from fantasies of incorporating the phallus of the powerful father or his equivalent, and they had to be defended against as well. The matter becomes more complicated when we consider that the motivation for defense comes from unpleasurable affect. At first we understood anxiety to be the instigator of defense (Freud, 1926), but later we came to accept that any unpleasant affect can evoke a defensive response from the ego (Brenner, 1974). Accordingly, in addition to defending against the aforementioned drive derivatives, the patient's ego had to defend against a sense of betrayal, depression, shame over weakness, shame over homosexual wishes, and guilt over hurtful behavior to his mother and brother in his childhood and to his wife and children in his adult life.

Guided by the structural model, a therapist might well construe his task to be the analysis of defense, leading to the exposure and resolution of these many conflicts. Conceptually, this understanding of what the therapist is trying to do is clearly different from the task a therapist guided by the schema model sets for himself. If the psychopathology is understood as the presence of an active, sequestered schema organized around the traumata of the past, then clearly the therapeutic task is to enable the patient to recognize the existence and activity of such an organization; to see how pervasive, often in subtle ways, are its influences on his mental set, perceptions, and behavior; and to enable him to struggle to erode the disruptive effects of this schema and replace the continual acting out of old tableaus with mature, adaptive reason and judgment.

In the case of the senior athlete described in Chapter Four, it was noted that with the realization that the problem was one of dealing not with a number of discrete issues including aggression, sibling rivalry, and self-esteem, but with an organization made up of the traumatic experience, reactive fantasies, and associated affects of the patient's fifth year, a shift in therapeutic focus occurred. Though we continued to analyze transference manifestations, dreams, and other derivatives, the understandings achieved were regarded not as ends in themselves but as facets of a pathogenic organization. Insights now tended to fit into a dynamic scheme and to reinforce one another. As treatment progressed, the shape and content of this organization became more clear, its manifestations ego dystonic. The patient was able to make an increasingly sharp delineation between his ego or adult self and the freeze-frame of his fifth year. This distinction between the adult making his way in life and the troubled, traumatized child is a consequence of a therapeutic approach that views the pathology as arising from the disruptive activity of a sequestered, nonaccommodating schema. It is fostered by the use of interpretations that encompass the traumatic nidus and several of the elements of the pathogenic organization. In Chapter Four, two kinds of conflictual interface were distinguished: one within the pathogenic schema and one between the pathogenic schema and the ego. Interpretations that address the former kind of interface might be called *single impulse/single defense* interpretations; interpretations that address the latter kind of interface might be called *en bloc* interpretations.

To return to the example of the attorney, during a Monday session he reported that he felt unaccountably depressed. His remarks led him to recount that he and his family had spent the previous day visiting his close friend. His friend had used the occasion to tell him how much money he had made in the year that had just ended. The patient had become immediately jealous but quickly put aside this feeling as being an unworthy reaction to his friend's good fortune. As he went on, he compared his own uncertain prospects with the other's situation. It was evident that he had suppressed his anger and his wishes to deprive his friend but that these feelings were alive in him and accounted for his depressed mood. An interpretation addressed to this interface is a single impulse single/defense interpretation. Such interpretations are part of the everyday work of insight-oriented psychotherapies.

During another session, the patient disparaged himself for being so clinging to his wife, and it occurred to him that he typically rushed home from work at the earliest feasible moment. He wondered if he were afraid she would not be there. He was annoyed that he often lost control and screamed at his sons and that his wife would see this and disapprove and at times come to the boys' rescue. He wondered why he was so desperate to achieve great success in business, for he was actually secure financially. It occurred to him that he had to prove his worth, that otherwise he might be cast aside as a loser, a nothing. My interventions in this instance were designed to help him see how he was reliving the childhood situation in which he was afraid his mother would disappear or that he would lose her love and regard, in which he hated his rivals, and in which he was desperate to prove his value. The patient was able to see that the various matters he had brought up derived from the organized residue of a traumatic period of his life, that he was remaking an old movie. Interpretations addressed to this interface were en bloc interpretations.

According to the schema model, the therapeutic process enables the adaptive, objective aspect of the patient, the ego, to become aware of the content and activity of the disruptive residues of his traumatic past (pathogenic schema). It follows that the therapist consistently addresses the ego while exploring the pathogenic schema with the patient. From time to time, I have treated patients who had extended prior therapies in which a great deal of the past was uncovered with limited improvement. In one instance, according to the patient, the previous therapist was always seeking to have the patient reexperience "the next lower level" in order to effect a "cure." Another patient entered treatment during a crisis and sobbed uncontrollably during the first visit. At our second meeting, feeling much better, the patient remarked how helpful it was that I had tried to identify what had precipitated the crisis and why it had had such a profound effect rather than to dwell on his feelings of despair, as he had anticipated from past experience. Another patient made a distinction between "wallowing in the past" and seeking to understand and gain mastery over it.

In making this point we are being consistent with the structural model, which regards the ego as the central mediating part of the psyche. Nonetheless, some therapists, without addressing or paying heed to an objective, observing ego, seek to have their patients regress endlessly. They are engaged in cathartic treatments, and, assuming a strict adherence to their model, it is difficult to see how they can bring treatments to satisfactory terminations. It may be that, for such therapists, the dynamic unconscious is an infinite morass that can never be plumbed satisfactorily, rather than an organization that can be understood and worked through if not to the point of extinguishing the pain, then at least approaching that point asymptotically.

The Functioning of the Therapist in the Treatment Situation

While the questions of how the therapist functions in the treatment situation and the nature of the nontransference relationship between the patient with the therapist are not specific to the schema model, they do deserve mention in a discussion of treatment. Greenson and Wexler (1969) expressed the hope that their paper had stimulated further discussion of the nontransference relationship. The issue of the nontransference relationship has as its immediate corollary the question, how should the therapist behave within the treatment situation so as to advance the treatment most efficaciously? Although the basic requirements for the therapist's neutrality and relative anonymity seem clear, discussions of these and other aspects of the general functioning of the analyst often arouse controversy.

Attempts at such discussions have often contrasted the analyst as a human being, with habits, foibles, feelings, with the analyst as mirror, research scientist, or schematic perfectionist in carrying out the principle of abstinence. For example, Fenichel (1941) wrote:

> One analyst wished to forbid analysts to smoke in order that they might be *exclusively* a "mirror." I have often been surprised at the frequency with which I hear from patients who had previously been in analysis with another analyst, that they were astonished at my "freedom" and "naturalness" in analysis. They had believed that an analyst is a special creation and is not permitted to be human! Just the opposite impression should prevail. The patient should always be able to rely on the "humanness" of the analyst [p. 74].

Greenson (1965) wrote:

> All analysts recognize the need for deprivations in psychoanalysis; they would also agree in principle on the analyst's need to be human. The problem arises, however, in determining what is meant by humanness in the analytic situation and how does one reconcile this with the principle of deprivation. Essentially the humanness of the analyst is expressed in his compassion, concern, and therapeutic intent toward his patient. It matters to him how the patient fares, he is not just an observer or a research worker. He is a physician or a therapist, and his aim is to help the patient get well. . . . Humanness is also expressed in the attitude that the patient is to be respected as an individual [p. 178].

And Stone (1961) wrote:

> On re-examination of original precepts and the development of traditional practices, one is confronted by an important question: may not the trend toward a schematic perfection in carrying out the principle of abstinence and allied technical precepts have overwhelmed awareness of the reservations supplied by common sense and intuitive

> wisdom from the beginning, and thus subtly and inadvertently produced superfluous technical difficulties of a paradoxical character? The tendencies I have in mind are the withholding or undue limitation of certain legitimate and well-controlled gratifications, which can provide a palpably human context for the transmission of understanding, which is . . . the central function of the analyst [pp. 107–108].

The concept of the therapeutic alliance (Zetzel, 1956, 1966) or the working alliance (Greenson, 1965) has come to stand in general terms for the cooperative nontransference relationship between patient and therapist. Curtis (1979), however, while acknowledging the value of studying the collaborative aspect of analysis, was concerned lest there be a shift of focus away from intrapsychic conflict and the interpretation of transference and resistance toward viewing the therapeutic alliance as a new and corrective object relation, an end in itself. Brenner (1979) reviewed the papers by Zetzel and Greenson and questioned Zetzel's theoretical notion that the analytic relationship has as its basis the patient's original relationship to his or her mother. Further, he examined the clinical material offered by Zetzel and Greenson to exemplify the therapeutic alliance and demonstrated persuasively that these authors had overlooked dynamic factors and had not made a strong case for the concept. It was his view that

> when a patient *is* in analysis, the better one understands his resistances and the more knowledgably one is able to interpret their determinants to him, the better the chance that the patient can cooperate constructively. Whether at the beginning, in the midst, or in the final stages of analysis, timely, accurate interpretations that are based on correct understanding are far more useful in promoting a patient's ability to do his part than is any behavior, however well intentioned, humane, and intuitively compassionate, that is intended to make him feel less withdrawn, uncomfortable, or antagonistic [p. 150].

And further

> I believe that an analyst's human responsibility to his patients is to understand them as best he can and to convey to them what he understands for their benefit [p. 154].

We subscribe entirely to these views. The therapeutic, or working, alliance as it was originally conceptualized is a perversion of the therapeutic relationship and provides a theoretical basis for the therapist who is having difficulty understanding what is happening with his patient to shift his efforts from analysis of the patient's material to manipulation of the relationship. Clearly, the therapist's function is to understand the warded-off, anachronistic material at the root of his patient's illness and to communicate these understandings to the patient in a manner that will enable the patient to reduce or eliminate the disruptive effects of this residue of his traumatic past. It has occurred in practice that a patient complains that he or she feels like a puzzle being solved or even "a frog pinned to a board for dissection"; the therapist is not experienced at being caring or sympathetic. Or, in another instance, a patient proclaimed that the working out of her childhood dynamics was not the essential factor in her considerable improvement ("not half of it"), but, rather, was the caring, sympathetic therapeutic approach. These reactions are manifestations of difficulties, generally prephallic, that the patients had with childhood objects. In these instances, as with other transference reactions, the therapist might consider what recently occurred in the treatment situation and what is going on currently in the patient's life against the background of the past; the therapist would then be in a position to help the patient to understand what is being reexperienced and how it relates to the pathogenic residue of the patient's past.

We conceive the proper and efficacious behavior of the therapist along the lines Lichtenberg and I (1977) laid out some years ago; this study also took up the nature of the therapeutic relationship that evolves as a consequence of the therapist's behavior. In reviewing this material, we are not suggesting a change in or contribution to technique; we are attempting to make explicit certain processes that occur in the course of psychoanalysis and psychoanalytically oriented psychotherapy.

The therapist listens to the patient from several frames of reference, at times shifting from one to another, at times dwelling on a particular one. At times he listens to the patient as a person troubled by pathology but making his way in life, dealing with situations in his varied relationships, his vocation, his health, and whatever else occupies him. At other times he concentrates on a specific incident the patient reports, or a dream, or other derivative of the patient's underlying conflicts. At still other times he may focus on a silence or change of subject that suggests an interference with free association and the presence of resistance. He is alert to manifestations of transference. Yet another frame of reference is his own affective reactions to the patient's material which provide clues to the meaning of covert material or possibly to problems with his countertransference. Much could be said about each of these aspects of the therapist's listening, and the list is not exhaustive.

Since the therapist listens to his patient from many frames of reference and oscillates among them, his attentiveness requires special qualities. This kind of listening has generally been referred to as *evenly suspended attention*. Freud (1909) first used a similar phrase to refer to the need for the analyst to suspend prior judgment about the meaning of a symptom and instead give "impartial attention to everything that there is to observe" (p. 23). In 1912, Freud reiterated the warning against the analyst's deliberately concentrating his attention selectively on the basis of prior expectations. He added that the analyst should not attempt to fix material in his memory but should "give himself over completely to his 'unconscious memory' " (p. 112). Evenly suspended attention has as its function the taking in, resonating with, and conceptually ordering the communications of the patient; a second function is to formulate interventions that will be useful to the treatment, taking into account the patient's readiness to hear what is being pointed out and how the interventions might best be worded

Thus, the therapist listens to understand and to respond. This is what the rational side of the patient expects—that he be understood by the therapist, who will help him learn about himself. The usual functioning of the therapist is, in fact, a continuous form of communication in which he conveys a sense of therapeutic perceptiveness by being appropriately silent, retentive, and reflective, by being curious and interested, and by making his interventions in a tactful, understandable manner. Ideally he does so by performing these functions with a comfortable acceptance of those qualities which characterize his individual style. Thus he presents himself to the patient as a professional with purpose, method, and style, one who performs his functions while remaining an unobtrusive, unpretentious, non-self-centered object with whom the patient can explore his psychopathology. The therapeutic relationship exists between a helper and one who is being helped. Because the therapist shows a restricted part of himself and because the relationship is subject to the patient's assimilatory tendencies, a kind of "psychic suction" occurs "in which many of the past attitudes, specific experiences, and fantasies of the patient are re-enacted . . . with the analyst as the main figure of significance" (Greenacre, 1954, p. 675). At the same time, the patient's sense of how the analyst functions provides a stimulus for the patient to develop and employ a capacity for reflective self-awareness. In the previous chapter (in the section on working through) we referred to the patient's identification with the therapist's cognitive style and reality orientation.

Historically, it may have been essential for the development of psychoanalysis that stress be placed on the analyst's unobtrusiveness, rather than on other aspects of the analyst's personality or on his active responsive functions. Yet, in order for the treatment situation to have the emotional impact necessary to foster the development of an analyzable transference, the therapist must communicate his presence as an integral part of what he communicates through his functioning. It is not sufficient to have only the smile of the Cheshire cat; the face is also necessary. This presence will be experienced by the patient not only as a sense of therapist's helpful intent and participation, but also in terms of specific aspects of the therapist's personality.

For example, in his efforts to understand, the analyst might well reveal himself as curious and quick, or, at times, as dense; he might show that he gains some pleasure in discovery; that he can be patient yet persevering amid confusion; that he has attitudes and affects consistent with efforts at understanding enigmatic or puzzling situations. In communicating his understanding, (as opposed to, say, entertaining, conversing, moralizing), he may employ analogy, anecdote, humor, references to cultural mores, and the like. He may indicate sympathetic recognition of the patient's feelings of progress or lack of progress. In short, he reveals actual but circumscribed aspects of his self. Such revelations we regard not as undesirable contaminants but as necessary ingredients of the analytic situation. The therapist recognizes that elements of his personality may be received in different ways: they may be subject to perceptual distortion and to transference elaboration; or they may be perceived accurately and responded to without an associative link to the infantile conflict affecting the response. In any case, the analyst must accept the patient's scrutiny and must assume that what he communicates of his personality is itself a part of the analytic experience and a part of the patient's associational content.

As Anna Freud (quoted in Greenson and Wexler, 1969) put it:

> I have always learned to consider transference in the light of a distortion of the real relationship of the patient to the analyst, and of course, that the type and manner of distortion showed up the contributions from the past. If there were no real relationship this idea of the distorting influences would make no sense [p. 28].

Thus, in considering the general functioning of the therapist within the therapeutic situation, we are in agreement with Brenner (1979) in rejecting the concepts of therapeutic alliance and working alliance as they were first elaborated. We feel that the frequency with which these terms are encountered in the literature and in psychoanalytic discourse is attributable to their having lost their original meaning, and they now serve as handy expressions to designate the collaborative efforts of patient and therapist. We agree with Brenner that the therapist's role is to understand his patient and to communicate this understanding in a way that is helpful to the patient. As Brenner asserts, the therapist who functions in this way is being both human and humane if he is handling himself in the way most likely to relieve the patient's neurotic suffering.

We have, we believe, filled out this picture in two respects. First, we note that the patient not only benefits as the recipient of the therapist's interpretations, he also identifies with the therapist's ways of listening and his cognitive processing of the material. Such identifications are necessary for the patient to enter actively into the exploration of his own material and for the self-analytic work that may follow termination. Second, we take the position that the therapist may and should be human, in the sense of being natural, in expressing his own personality, while at the same time restricting himself to the proper functions of the therapist—namely, listening, understanding, and communicating the fruits of understanding.

CHAPTER SEVEN

◄ ►

The Schema Model and the Structural Model

In formulating the structural model, Freud (1923) explained that he had discarded the topographic model for two reasons. The first problem he had with the topographic model was the circumstance that the defenses of the ego were regularly unconscious. He wrote:

> We have come upon something in the ego itself which is also unconscious, which behaves exactly like the repressed, that is, which produces powerful effects without itself being conscious and which requires special work before it can be made conscious. From the point of view of analytic practice, the consequence of this piece of observation is that we land in endless confusion and difficulty if we cling to our former way of expressing ourselves and try, for instance, to derive neurosis from a conflict between the conscious and the unconscious. We shall have to substitute for this antithesis another, taken from our understanding of the structural conditions of the mind, namely, the antithesis between the organized ego and what is repressed and dissociated from it [p. 17].

This difficulty with the topographic model might have been dealt with simply by stating that the relationship to consciousness was not a consistent criterion by which to distinguish between the ego and what was warded off by the ego. Indeed, in classroom remarks Waelder during the 1960s repeatedly said that he could get along perfectly well with the topographic model, keeping in mind that the defensive activity of the ego was unconscious. The second reason Freud (1923) gave for abandoning the topographic model was his recognition that the feeling of guilt and the need for punishment may also be unconscious. Freud (1914) had already proposed that within the ego was a part called the ego ideal, or superego. This part of the ego was, of course, concerned with moral values and punishment for ethical violations. Again, the problem had to do with the relationship between consciousness and a part of the ego.

If these were the difficulties with the topographic model, the solution, namely, its replacement with the structural model, seems a radical one. The structural model entailed the concept of the id, which in 1923 was only vaguely defined as being the region of the mind from whence the instincts arise. The repressed, which is "cut off sharply from the ego by the resistances of repression. . . ," now became a part of the id. Later, Freud (1933) elaborated this concept extensively. Thus:

> It [the id] is the dark, inaccessible part of our personality; what we know of it we have learnt from our study of the dream-work and of the construction of neurotic symptoms, and most of that is of a negative character and can be described only as a contrast to the ego. We approach the id with analogies: we call it a chaos, a cauldron full of seething excitations. We picture it as being open at its end to somatic influences, and as there taking up into itself instinctual needs which find their psychical expression in it, but we cannot say in what substratum. It is filled with energy reaching it from the instincts, but it has no organization, produces no collective will, but only a striving to bring about the satisfaction of the instinctual needs subject to the observance of the pleasure principle. The logical laws of thought do not apply in the id, and this is true above all of the law of contradiction. Contrary impulses exist side by side, without canceling each other out or diminishing each other: at the most they converge to form

> compromises under the dominating economic pressure towards the discharge of energy [pp. 73–74].

Freud asserted that there is no negation in the id and that there is no appreciation of the passage of time. He went on:

> The id of course knows no judgments of value: no good and evil, no morality. The economic or, if you prefer, the quantitative factor, which is intimately linked to the pleasure principle, dominates all its processes. Instinctual cathexes seeking discharge—that, in our view, is all there is to the id. [p. 74].

Thus, one might say about the id that its mode of activity is primary process, that it is linked to the soma and is the seat of the instincts, and that it operates according to the pleasure principle. Schur (1966), who devoted a monograph to the concept, found that Freud's conceptualization of the id remained vague: "We have had to ask ourselves not only: 'What did Freud mean by this concept?' (p. 29) but even more important 'How can we fit these conceptualizations into the whole framework of our psychoanalytic theory and practice?' " (p. 29). The term has eluded crisp definition. Members of a panel (Marcovitz, 1963) on the topic could agree only on the presence of confusion and the need for clarification. Arlow summed up the discussion, according to the report, saying:

> Disagreements existed concerning the boundaries of the id and whether or not "formed elements" should be included. There were variations in emphasis between more biologically and more psychologically oriented theories. The panel was divided on the relationship of the structural and topographical frames of reference. Although there was agreement that both were useful and could be used simultaneously, there was disagreement about the necessity for separating the two sets of concepts completely, specifically relating to the question of separating the concept of the id from that of the unconscious. There was disagreement about concepts concerning perception and on how to delineate awareness of events relating to the id [p. 160].

Since Schur's (1966) monograph the concept has been little mentioned in the literature, and it seems to have dropped out of psychoanalytic discourse. A central component of the model as formulated by Freud is being ignored.

At this juncture it is worthwhile to repeat the discussion of primary process made earlier. As we noted the unconscious of the topographic model and the id of the structural model are characterized by fluidity; they use unbound energy and employ primary process. At the same time, the repressed is said to be fixed, perhaps unalterable. The repressed's resistance to change may thus explain the need for lengthy analysis. In accordance with the schema model, we agree with the position holding that the unconscious tends to be fixed. Primary-process thinking is , in our view, an interface phenomenon, a regressive form of cognition that appears in situations of conflict between the ego and the repressed. The same mechanisms at work in the primary-process mentation of the unconscious are also to be found in dream work and the defensive organization, both functions of the ego.

Further, the concept of the repressed or dynamic unconscious (or sequestered schema) has no clear, generally accepted relationship to the structural model. In spite of their central role in the structure of neuroses and in spite of the necessity for understanding them in the conduct of analyses, these schemas are not components of the basic model of the mind in current psychoanalytic theory, that is, the structural model. Not only are they not components of this model, but there is a great deal of confusion as to how they might be related to the model. Many analysts who are willing to concede this point are not upset by it because they view the structural model as only one of several models available, not as the basic model of the mind in the sense that it should subsume all other models and be compatible with all clinical data. A great many other analysts, probably the majority, do regard the structural model as the basic model in this sense. In any case, it is worthwhile to examine the ways in which these patterns of fantasy and memories have been related to the structural model.

In order to discuss this issue we must reiterate that what is referred to here as the sequestered schema has in other contexts been called the dynamic, or repressed, unconscious. In other words, these terms refer to organizations of memories, fantasies, traumatic events, theories of gender determination, and other elements that, by virtue of their pressure and activity, give rise to symptoms and other influences on a person's experience and behavior.

Freud (1939) contended that the repressed was a part of the ego relegated to the id.

> In the earliest period of life, while the ego is developing out of the id . . a portion of the contents of the id is taken into the ego and raised to the preconscious state; another portion is not affected by this translation and remains behind in the id as the unconscious proper. In the further course of the formation of the ego, however, certain psychical impressions and processes in the ego are excluded (i.e. expelled) from it by a defensive process: The characteristic of being preconscious is withdrawn from them, so that they are once more reduced to being component portions of the id. Here then is the "repressed" in the id [p. 96].

A similar exposition appears in "An Outline of Psychoanalysis" (Freud 1940, p. 163).

On the other hand, on the basis of definitions of the macrostructures generally agreed upon, a line of reasoning can be developed to show that the repressed is part of the ego.

> Karush then reasoned as follows: An instinct cannot be represented otherwise than by an idea. Ideas are derived ultimately from perceptions which become associated with word representations. "Psychic representatives" then are basically perceptions of the activity of instincts. Perceptions can be created only by the ego, of which the perceptual function is a part. Therefore the id can be regarded as a nonpsychic structure composed of biological forces, in which case the ego becomes a more inclusive organization that contains all repressed ideas and the psychic representatives of the instincts as well [Marcovitz, 1963, p. 152].

Still others would disagree both with the position taken by Freud (1939), who wrote that the repressed "is to be counted as belonging to the id" (p. 96) and with the position, here represented by Karush, that the ego "contains all repressed ideas." They would say that these positions betray the concept of the ego and id as containers and in this way harken back to the topographical model, which they regard as anathema. Among them—for we are dealing with a wide variety of opinions and understandings masked by a pseudoconsensus of allegiance to the structural model—are those who will point out that because these schemas are the product of the interactions of ego, id, and superego and as such are intersystemic, they cannot be part of the model of the mind but are instead products of the mind.

These positions certainly are tenable; each has many adherents. Yet clearly there are serious problems with each of them once it is recognized that these schemas are both intersystemic and parties to conflict. Because they are intersystemic, assigning them to any of the macrostructures must create a circularity of reasoning. Because they are parties to conflict and are indeed essential clinical data, it seems capricious to exclude them as components of the model. See Gill (1963) for an extensive treatment of these issues.

Still another difficulty with the structural model, as Klein (1976) and Stolorow (1978), among others, have pointed out, is that there is no clear, consistent definition of what is meant by structure in psychoanalytic discourse. There is ambiguity as to whether id, ego, and superego are to be regarded as merely classifications of functions enabling the clinician to organize the clinical data in situations of conflict or whether they refer to objectively existing, causally affective entities. If the former—that is, if the macrostructures merely refer to classes of functions useful for organizing psychoanalytic data—then they lack explanatory power and hardly constitute a model of the mind. As Stolorow (1978) points out, however, commingled

> with these clinically derived classifications are conceptions of the id, ego, and superego as "mental agencies"—literally existent structural entities which perform actions,

> bind, utilize and discharge energies, and contain specific contents within their boundaries [p. 314].

Stolorow goes on to note that these clearly metapsychological usages are replete with such conceptual errors as unlabeled metaphors, concretistic reifications of abstractions, tautological pseudoexplanations of behavior as being determined by hypothetical entities, personifications, and anthropomorphisms. In addition, there is no internally consistent way to define the three macrostructures (Slap, 1986) Slap and Saykin, 1983, 1984).

Unless, as sometimes happens in psychoanalysis, one makes a virtue of uncertainty and multiple understandings, it is difficult to comprehend the structural model. If the macrostructures contribute to behavior; that is, if they have effects, then they must be reified or anthropomorphized. If they are neither reified nor anthropomorphized, then they are indeed reduced to classifications of functions and as such fail to qualify as structures as the word is universally construed.

Schemas, on the other hand, are neither lifeless classifications nor reified metapsychological abstractions. They are clinically inferable organizations of memories, patterns of fantasy, motives, knowledge, theories, moral values, and so forth. As such, the activity of schemas remains distinctly human and the comprehension of this activity involves neither anthropomorphism of structures (e.g., cruel superego) nor dehumanization, as seems inevitable with the tripartite model.

Another problematic area of the structural model is perception. Two aspects of Freud's treatment of perception have had profound consequences for the structural model. The first of these has always been taken for granted and has not been the focus of critical attention. This is Freud's attribution of perception to a particular part or organization of the psychic apparatus through which stimuli from the outside must pass and be subject to modification before reaching other parts. The second, which has been the subject of critical reexamination (Beres and Joseph, 1970; Schimek, 1975) is his treatment of perception as a true and accurate copy, much like a photograph, of external reality rather than as a process that depends on internal organizations involving past experience, cognitive functioning, and dynamic and affective processes.

First, the locus of perception. According to the topographic model, perceptions enter the psychic apparatus by way of the unconscious (Freud, 1915):

> Normally all the paths from perception to the Ucs. remain open, and only those leading on from the Ucs. are subject to blocking and repression.
>
> It is a very remarkable thing that the Ucs. of one human being can react upon that of another, without passing through the Cs [p. 194].

The passage of perceptions from the Ucs. to Pcs. and Cs. is not a free and simple process, for there are repressive barriers between the systems. It is necessary for a presentation in the Ucs. to acquire a word presentation in order to become preconscious.

> The system Ucs. contains the thing-cathexes of the objects, the first and true object-cathexes; the system Pcs. comes about by this thing-presentation being bypercathected through being linked with the word-presentations corresponding to it [pp. 201–202].

In "The Ego and the Id" (Freud, 1923), however, one reads, "All perceptions which are received from without (sense perceptions) . . . are Cs. from the start" (p. 19).[1] Freud's diagram of the psychic apparatus (p. 24) makes clear that perception is a function of the ego and is linked to consciousness in that the perceptual system (Pcpt.) is joined with the Cs. to form Pcpt.-

[1]While a major thesis of "The Ego and the Id" was that much of the activity of the ego took place outside of consciousness, Freud was quite clear that perception took place on a conscious level. He reiterated this understanding in "A Note on the Mystic Writing Pad" (1925), in which he stated that the functions of perception and memory were divided among separated but interrelated systems: "The layer which receives the stimuli—the system Pcpt.-Cs.—forms no permanent trace; the foundations of memory come about in other adjoining systems" (p. 230).

Cs., which constitutes the ego's surface, that is, its interface with the external world. The repressed unconscious is now part of the id, which is "cut off from the external world" (Freud, 1940, p. 198).

Thus, we see that, according to the topographic model, the perception of external stimuli takes place in the unconscious layers of the mind and rises to preconscious and conscious layers by attaching word presentations. The structural model turns things around, in that perception now takes place at the most conscious level, the Pcpt.-Cs., and is sharply cut off from the unconscious layers.

To be sure, problems exist in the theory of perception within the framework of the topographic model; for example, the distinction between thing-presentations and word-presentations has not proven useful and has dropped out of theoretical discourse. It is, however, the treatment of perception from the perspective of the structural model that commands our attention. There are difficulties with the idea that perception is a function of the conscious ego (Pcpt.-Cs.) and that there is no direct perceptual pathway to the unconscious layers of the mind. It is an everyday observation in analytic practice that people react to seductive, hostile, and other behaviors by others without recognizing these behaviors consciously. Registration of tachistoscopic and other subliminal stimuli is demonstrable under experimental conditions. More troublesome for this theory is the problem of accounting for the stimulation of unconscious drive derivatives, guilt, and other elements of intrapsychic conflict by the events of the external world. If the ego stands between the external world and the repressed, why does it not block these percepts from the repressed? If instead the ego is unable to function in this way and percepts have an easy path to the repressed, what is gained by maintaining that the id is cut off from the external world? Arlow (1969a) has tried to deal with this issue as follows:

> There is a mutual and reciprocal effect of the pressure of unconscious fantasy formations and sensory stimuli, especially stimuli emanating from the external world. Unconscious fantasy activity provides the "mental set" in which

> sensory stimuli are perceived and integrated. External events, on the other hand, stimulate and organize the re-emergence of unconscious fantasies. In keeping with its primitive nature, the basic fantasy is cathected with a highly mobile energy, and presses for gratification of the sort which Freud characterized as tending toward an identity of perception. The pressure may affect many functions of the ego. Derivatives of fantasies may influence ego functions, interfering, for example, with the neutral processes of registering, apperceiving, and checking the raw data of perception. Under the pressure of these influences, the ego is oriented to scan the data of perception and to select discriminatively from the data of perception those elements that demonstrate some consonance or correspondence with the latent preformed fantasies [p. 8].

A complicated sequence is described here. Arlow states that "external events . . . stimulate and organize the reemergence of unconscious fantasies"; he thus seems to concede a perceptual capacity to the unconscious fantasy organizations in contradiction to the idea that perception is exclusively an ego function. The fantasies thus stimulated press for gratification and influence the ego to select discriminatively from the data of perception those elements that demonstrate "some consonance or correspondence" with the latent, preformed fantasies. Some questions are raised by this sequence; for example, if the fantasy formations perceive, that is, if they are stimulated by external events that have significance for them, why must they influence the ego to search ("scan the data of perception") for elements that demonstrate consonance or correspondence with the fantasy formations themselves?

Given these clinical and theoretical difficulties for the current theory of the locus and flow of perception in the structural model, would it not be more reasonable to attribute a perceptual capacity to both psychic organizations, that is, to the ego and to the repressed? It is true that this alteration in theory entails the surrender of the idea consistently held by Freud that perceptions enter the psychic apparatus by way of a particular portal, an idea that possibly has its origins in Freud's early concept of neurosis as arising from an interference in a reflex arc between stimulation and discharge (Breuer and Freud, 1893–1895). The psychic apparatus, however, is a model of the mind, not an anatomical entity equipped with sense organs; whether sensory data, mediated by the brain, become available to only one, or to more than one, psychic organization is a matter to be decided by clinical considerations.

In regard to Freud's view of perception as a true and accurate copy of external reality, Beres and Joseph (1970) and Schimek (1975), in papers on the concept of the mental representation, have addressed the way perception is treated in psychoanalytic theory. Schimek, in a critical reexamination of Freud's view on cognition, wrote:

> For Freud, in line with the association theory of the 19th century, perception is essentially the passive, temporary registration of a specific external object. The perceptual apparatus functions like the lens of a camera. In order to keep its unlimited receptive capacity for new registrations, it retains no permanent traces of them; it is "without the capacity to retain modifications and thus without memory" (1900, p. 539). This means that perception is uninfluenced by past experience and not subject to a developmental and learning process. Freud often equates the two terms "perception" and "external reality" and uses them interchangeably. Such a view (sometimes labeled a "copy" theory of knowledge or the principle of "immaculate perception") implies an innate capacity for veridical objective registration of discrete external objects, and a direct and intrinsic correspondence between the "real" external object and the perception of it [pp. 172–173].

Beres and Joseph presented a more modern view of perception than Freud's: the sense organs are stimulated by the external world and its objects and the resultant excitations are processed by the central nervous system to create a world of perception and ideation. Each individual has his own reality, which consists not of the raw data of the stimuli impinging on the sense organs, but rather of the mental representations activated by these stimuli. These mental representations are influenced by drive constellations, affective states, past experience, and cognitive considerations. Beres and Joseph postulated that a mental representation consists of an unconscious organization. Further, they acknowledged (p. 2, fn. 2) that at the time they were writing, the concept of the schema to characterize such mental organizations was receiving more attention in the psychological literature and there was increasing recognition in the psychoanalytic literature of the holistic aspect of experience and psychic activity.

These remarks concerning the implication of Freud's assumptions about perception for the structural model pertain, of course, to that version of the model advanced in 1923 and not to its evolution under the aegis of the ego psychologists. Actually if one corrects for these assumptions—that is, if one assumes that both the ego and the repressed have perceptual capabilities (which differ in their respective cognitive characteristics)—and if one recognizes that conscious perception is not a photographic imaging of external reality but the result of the activity of mental representations that are influenced by drive constellations, affective states, past experience and cognitive factors, then one arrives at a model of the mind essentially congruent with the schema model.

The application of the tripartite model to clinical material, in the view of many, tends to dissect the patient in ways that are not helpful. In a summary of a discussion group on the current status of the structural theory, Frattaroli (1984) noted, that there was a widespread feeling that the structural theory is not especially relevant to clinical work and could even interfere with the analyst's awareness of the patient as person. Analysts may understand a patient in terms of a variety of disparate conflicts between the macrostructures or stemming from divers drives—for instance, problems with passivity, homosexuality, and aggression—without an appreciation that the clinical manifestations they are interpreting as separate issues are actually derivatives of the patient's sequestered schema and are, as such, elements in that pattern of fantasy. For example, an oedipal boy exposed to the primal scene might develop a number of fantasies in reaction to this trauma. He might deny his smallness and imagine himself a superhero; he might wish for a powerful male who would provide him with phallic supplies; he might wish to castrate the father in order to incorporate his phallus; he might identify with the mother, at once achieving intimacy with her and avoiding a battle with the father. Is the clinician better off seeing separate problems with narcissism, homosexuality, aggression, and feminine identity, or is he better off understanding the nature of the trauma and the way the little boy attempted to cope with it? As Frattaroli (1984) put it:

> Are patients more likely to benefit from understanding their problems in terms of forbidden (superego) impulses, wishes and ideas (id) which are warded off in various symptomatic and characterologic ways (ego), or do they find it more helpful to understand how they are driven continually to reenact and recreate a schema, scenario, or personal version of reality, a story about their relationship to the world of significant others; and to remember the traumatic events and relations which could not be integrated by the relatively immature psyche and thus gave rise to the schema? [p. 9].

Apfelbaum (1965) pointed out that Freud's theoretical energy conceptions seem to enjoy a certain immunity; that is, they continue to be honored and accepted in spite of significant criticism, although in the quarter century following Apfelbaum's observation, the importance attached to energy concepts by the analytic mainstream has diminished. Such is not the case with the structural model, which continues to be the central paradigm for psychoanalytic teaching and thought. As it has become more and more imprecise and difficult to defend, one begins to hear a little less about the structural *model*, and the terms *structural hypothesis* and, simply, *structure* appear more frequently. Apfelbaum suggested that this apparent immunity may be a consequence of the metapsychological approach that asserts that there are several points of view, namely, structural, economic, dynamic, genetic, and adaptive, which must all be considered if one hopes to understand psychoanalytic material completely or even satisfactorily. Pointing out the deficiencies of the structural model, therefore, has no persuasive force. This easy tolerance for the deficiencies of the central paradigm of dynamic psychology makes it difficult for the field to arrive at a paradigm that accounts for clinical data more precisely while correcting for the vagueness of the concepts and the internal consistencies of the structural model. The model, as Reiser (1984) has pointed out, is in a theoretical cul de sac.

A more formidable obstacle to change lies in the authoritarian tradition of psychoanalytic institutions. Freud was a towering figure, who during his lifetime essentially dominated the field. With his passing, the mantle of theoretical authority was assumed by Anna Freud and Hartmann, Kris, and Loewenstein. More recently, Arlow and Brenner have occupied an analagous position. Whereas in most institutions of learning, power is divided among administration, a board of directors, and faculty, in psychoanalytic institutes a small group of persons have tended to serve in all capacities. As a consequence, no system of checks and balances exists. Instead, psychoanalytic institutes are governed by benign oligarchic despots, politically powerful figures who have a great deal to say about who advances and who does not. Since it is difficult to know what actually goes on in any practitioner's office and since analysts deal with soft data and concepts of varying levels of abstraction, many judgments are made on a necessarily subjective basis. The nature of hierarchies within psychoanalytic institutions has led to a situation where many candidates have been forced, knowingly or unknowingly, into a passive acceptance of theory and to working within the existing paradigm, flawed though it may be. Creating, or even giving objective consideration to, alternatives may be damaging to one's career. It is to be hoped that as the number of nonmedical psychoanalytic candidates grows, we will see a change in the climate of these institutes. In doctoral training, students are encouraged to be innovative, to contribute something new. The training in medical school is necessarily far more authoritarian.

CHAPTER EIGHT

◄ ►

The Schema Model and the Self

The concept of self is an elusive one. No definition of the self seems to suffice; there are always common usages of the term that are not covered by any proposed definition, except, perhaps, that the self refers to one's totality, one's physical being and mental processes. But this definition is of little help in the study of psychodynamic science; it is merely a synonym for the person. This situation has been described by Schafer (1968):

> The referents of self in psychoanalytic writing are unclear and have no consensus behind them. Sometimes, self seems to refer to the aggregate of the more general or schematic self representations; sometimes, it seems to refer to an assumed (but never empirically demonstrated) synthesis or internal consistency of all self representations; sometimes, self refers to the sense of personal continuity or "identity"; and sometimes, it seems to be synonymous with organism, personality, something unspecified that lies behind all subjective experience, or another regulatory system that is superordinate, coordinate, or subordinate to id, ego, and superego.
>
> At present, therefore, the concept self is too diffuse and too resistant to standardized usage to be useful in metapsychological discussion [p. 27].

George Klein (1976) used the term self, or self-schema, to mean what we have called ego in the schema model. He pointed out that, as had been recognized by psychoanalytic structural theory, "conflict occurs only in relation to an integrating organization that is capable of *self*-observation, *self*-criticism, and choice, and that can regulate emotional needs and their expression" (p. 171). He argued that since classical theory at times sees the ego as the locus and resolver of conflict and at other times as a *party* to conflict (e.g., between an ego aim and a drive), some organization *beyond* or superordinate to the ego must be conceptualized to provide for integration of aims and adjudication of contradictions. Thus, he said, "the notion of *self* . . . now seems indispensable" (p. 172).

Klein conceived of the self as active in regard to the problems it confronts—both in resolving the demands made on it and in initiating purposes of its own. He cited as an early exposition of this position Waelder's (1936) view that the ego is not simply a passive mechanistic switchboard, but has "its own peculiar activity" (p. 47), that is, "an active trend toward the instinctual life, a disposition to dominate, or more correctly, to incorporate it into its organization" (pp. 47–48). For Klein, the synthetic function has the purpose of helping the person to maintain integrity among conscious aims, motives, and values; and the self is the source of this feeling of integrity. The sense of self has two aspects in dynamic equilibrium. One is individuality—"an autonomous unit, distinct from others as a locus of action and decision" (Klein 1976, p. 178); the other is "we-ness"—"one's self construed as a necessary part of a unit transcending one's autonomous actions" (p. 178). An example of "we-ness" is oneself as part of a family, community, or profession.

Klein's formulation of the concept of the self is not, in our view, compellingly different from previous usages of the ego concept. That, according to classical theory, the ego at times may be seen to resolve conflicts and at other times oppose drive tendencies does not appear to necessitate a concept of a superordinate organization; one could as easily say that the ego is the superordinate organization and has divers functions. In support of his argument for a concept of self superordinate to the ego, Klein adduces functions attributed to the ego, the synthetic function and the activity of the ego described by Waelder (1936), in the *Principle of Multiple Function*. When Klein turns to subjective experience as a manifestation of his concept of self, his argument loses credibility. The idea that the self is an autonomous unit that is the locus of action and decision ignores the contribution of unconscious determinants that arise from past traumata and from unresolved conflicts to conscious experience and behavior, as does his contention that the self is the source of a feeling of integrity among conscious aims, motives, and values.

In *Schizoid Phenomena, Object Relations and the Self* Guntrip (1969) presents a model of the mind influenced by Fairbairn and Winnicott. According to this model, the psyche consists initially of a pristine ego that seeks a secure relationship with a growth-promoting object. In reaction to painful experiences, this ego undergoes splitting; since such experiences are inevitable, splitting occurs in everyone but varies greatly from individual to individual. As a result of splitting, the ego gives off a central ego and an antilibidinal ego, leaving the libidinal ego, which is the true heart of the personality or the self. Under unfavorable circumstances this libidinal ego may undergo a further split in which a part, the regressed ego, seeks withdrawal to a state of absolute passive dependence. As Guntrip writes, this is "*a final split in the infantile ego which permits a most secret hidden core of the self to regress completely into what is probably an unconscious hallucinated reproduction of the intrauterine condition*" (p. 88). In this way Guntrip accounts for schizoid phenomena. The three major parts of the ego in this model are roughly equivalent to the macrostructures of the structural theory. The libidinal ego, or self, is a concept that resembles the repressed unconscious and replaces the id. The central ego is adaptive and compliant to the demands of reality and is the equivalent of the ego of structural theory; under unfavorable circumstances, it dominates the personality and becomes the false self. The antilibidinal ego is essentially identical to the superego.

Thus, we see that in contrast to Klein, whose concept of the self is analagous to some meanings of the ego, Guntrip, places it in the id. For Klein, the self is a superordinate structure, whereas for Guntrip it is a fragile structure whose growth relies on proper mothering.

Winnicott (1965) differentiates the self from the ego:

> It will be seen that the ego offers itself for study long before the word self has relevance. The word self arrives after the child has begun to use the intellect to look at what others see or feel or hear and what they conceive of when they meet this infant body [p. 56].

Winnicott has much more to say about the false self (central ego of the Guntrip model) than he does about the true self. Thus: "there is but little point in formulating a True Self idea except for the purpose of trying to understand the False Self, because it does no more than collect together the details of the experience of aliveness" (p. 148), and "the True Self appears as soon as there is any mental organization at all, and it means little more than the summation of sensori-motor aliveness" (p. 149). For Winnicott, the True Self must be carefully nurtured and is therefore initially totally dependent on the mother:

> . . . the infant develops an ego-organization that is adapted to the environment; but this does not happen automatically and indeed it can only happen if first the True Self (as I call it) has become a living reality, because of the mother's good enough adaptation to the infant's living needs [p. 149].

For Winnicott, it seems, the self is an elusive concept more or less equivalent to the "soul." Dependent on good-enough mothering for its development and vulnerable to injury from traumatic experience, the self is not a superordinate structure.

With the publication of *The Analysis of the Self* in 1971 Kohut established self psychology as a separate body of theory and therapeutic recommendations within psychoanalysis. Originally restricted to narcissistic personality disorders, self psychology has gradually extended its scope to the point where those who consider themselves self psychologists take an approach to their patients different from that of mainstream or orthodox analysts whatever the pathology. I have been critical of the theoretical basis for self psychology (Slap and Levine, 1978) and of the way it deals with dreams (Slap and Trunnell, 1987).

The earlier paper dealt with concepts that combined observable data with abstract hypothetical constructs; since the observable components were experience near, these hybrid concepts took on a spurious reality. As was pointed out, central to Kohut's (1971) teaching is the concept that the psychopathology of narcissistic personality disorders is caused by the realistic perception of the dangers of psychic trauma given certain deficiencies in ego structures and the presence of overwhelming excesses of primitive energy. Since the essence of the problem was felt to be in the failure of the formation of ego apparatuses, patients' complaints of feelings of defectiveness and inferiority were expressive of actual defectiveness of ego apparatuses. In this way, Kohut explained symptomatology on the basis of economic and hypothetical structural concepts. Further, therapeutic prescriptions were aimed at building structures rather than bringing to the patient's awareness knowledge of the pathogenic residues of his childhood in the expectation that working through this material would lead to increasing mastery and health. The 1987 paper noted that self psychologists believe that patients with narcissistic personality disorders have dreams that cannot be understood in the usual way and that these dreams, called self-state dreams, have a different origin and structure. The manifest content of these dreams is said to reveal the reactions of healthy sectors of the psyche to disturbing changes in the condition of the self. Self psychologists maintain that associations do not lead to hidden layers of the mind but that such dreams may be correctly interpreted by taking into account the patient's vulnerability and the situations leading to the intrusions of archaic material. Thus, in his efforts to interpret these dreams, the self psychologist does not search for day residue, nor is he concerned with the sources of various dream details; rather, by virtue of his empathy and his knowledge of the state of the patient's self, he is able to understand the dream directly as a portrayal of the dreamer's dread of threats to the integrity of his self. It was observed that, given that the self psychologists argue for a major revision in dream psychology, remarkably little had been published on self-state dreams.

Kernberg (1974) agrees with Kohut on the clinical characteristics of narcissistic personalities but holds different views on metapsychological assumptions and treatment. He feels that narcissistic personalities constitute a variant of borderline personality organization. The feature that sets narcissistic personality apart is the presence of an integrated, although highly pathological, grandiose self, reflecting a condensation of the real self, the ideal self, and the ideal object. It is a product of splitting; the borderline patient develops positive and negative identificatory systems, the former consisting of the ideal self and object, with associated positive affects, and the latter of the bad self and object, with associated negative affects. The structures and phenomena Kohut described, according to Kernberg, are a form of the positive identificatory system. Therefore, he disagrees with Kohut "about the origin of this grandiose self and whether it reflects the fixation of an archaic "normal" primitive self (Kohut's view) or a pathological structure, clearly different from normal infantile narcissism" (p. 257).

How does the body of theory and therapeutic recommendations of self psychology relate to the schema model? The schema model is a bipartite model. It consists of the ego, or unitary schema, and the sequestered potentially, if not actually, pathogenic residues from the past. The pathology Kohut described must lie, according to this model, either in the ego or in the sequestered material. Our view coincides with Kernberg's (1974); that is, the pathology described by the self psychologists is expressive of the pathogenic residues of failures in the early mother-child relationship. Kohut attempted to describe the same areas of pathological development addressed by Fairbairn, Guntrip, and Winnicott, among others. He did so in a more detailed and thorough manner, and his emphasis on empathy has been accepted as a valuable contribution even, as we shall see later, by some who do not entirely accept his theoretical position. Kohut (1984) wrote:

> How does self psychology perceive the process of cure? . . . the essential [step] defines the aim and the result of the cure—is the opening of a path of empathy between self and object, specifically, the establishment of empathic in-tuneness between self and self object on mature adult levels. This new channel of empathy permanently takes the place of the formerly repressed or split-off archaic narcissistic relationship; it supplants the bondage that had formerly tied the archaic self to the archaic self-object [pp. 65–66].

This statement seems to address essentially what Guntrip (1969) addresses in his discussions of the treatment of schizoid conditions and Winnicott (1965) in his dealing with the false self. It is consonant with the schema model as well, in the sense that what is repressed or split off by the ego is not a drive derivative but a far more complicated organization, in Kohut's terms, the archaic narcissistic relationship. Thus, we see this pathology as belonging to the sequestered organization; the consequence of the activity of this organization is that current relationships, events, and situations are cognitively processed according to the templates established at a time of great cognitive immaturity.

Self psychology posits a superordinate self-concept that in explanatory power supplants the mental agencies of the structural model (P. E. Stepansky, 1990, personal communication). According to the structural model, the ego would qualify as a superordinate agency since its function is to mediate between the demands of the id, the superego, and external reality. Yet just as the self is an elusive concept, the notion of a superordinate agency of the mind is difficult to pin down. When one considers the variety of pathological conditions there always seem to be exceptions to the idea of a superordinate agency. For example, every day people act out inappropriately and destructively in reaction to a stimulus that is anachronistically misinterpreted. It is difficult to account for a superordinate agency in fugue states and in multiple personality disorders. One may agree with Muslin (1985) that "the complete self is a superordinate structure, which functions not only as a receiver of impressions derived from the environment but as the center of action. It is experienced as continuous in space and time, as a center of action'' (p. 208). But this view of a superordinate self applies only in health and is the result of a complex developmental process.

In considering the role of empathy in psychoanalytic cure, Kohut (1984) asks whether the empathy of the psychoanalytic self psychologist is in essence different from that of analysts before the advent of self psychology and whether self psychologists achieve a cure through a novel kind of empathy. Though he feels that his answers to both questions are in principle negative, he does state that some of his self psychology colleagues would not agree, and he sketches out their anticipated objections, which he shares up to a point. He writes:

> These colleagues will . . . claim that in the clinical practice of psychoanalytic self psychology, in contrast to the clinical of practice of traditional psychoanalysis, the analyst truly grasps the patient's perception of his psychic reality and accepts it as valid. This is tantamount to saying that the self psychologist does not confront the patient with an ''objective'' reality that is supposedly more ''real'' than his inner reality, but rather confirms the validity and legitimacy of the patient's own perception or reality, however contrary it might be to the accepted view of reality held by most adults and by society at large [p. 173].

He makes a large point of such confrontations and characterizes them as often trite, superfluous, patronizing, and harmful to the progress of the analysis. They may momentarily enhance the analyst's self-esteem while shocking the patient.

Here Kohut may have raised a straw man; but, since it is not traditional analysis, but analysis based on the proposed schema model, that is under consideration, we shall not contest his characterization of how traditional analysts might behave. The therapist conducting a treatment guided by the schema model would seek to determine the nature of the pathogenic schema underlying the patient's illness. He would try to fathom the traumatic relationships and circumstances at the core of this organization as well as the associated affects and fantasies and other elements. Assuming that the therapist is a skilled and humane individual, he or she will necessarily be empathic as the patient's material is absorbed.

An apparent point of divergence appears, however, in the foregoing quoted passage, where Kohut claims that the self psychologist confirms the validity and legitimacy of the patient's own perception of reality, however contrary it is to an objective view of reality. We cannot agree that this is a logical or helpful position. For example; a professional man, a widower in his mid-forties, entered analysis in a near panic concerned with his competence and self-worth. He had left one firm as a consequence of a reorganization and now found that he was responsible to two superiors as he had two different areas of responsibility. He experienced one superior, a woman, as hostile and critical—interested only in having her needs served. The other, a man, was passive and distant, leaving the patient with a sense of being unrecognized and unappreciated. He was painfully insecure and would spend much of his spare time calling friends and relatives often pouring out his worries. In the analysis he strove to be a good patient, promising to accomplish various things and bringing in material he imagined I would appreciate.

It soon became apparent that this well-educated and generally estimable man was perceiving his current situation and living his life according to templates established early in his life. Having a cold and critical mother whom he could never seem to please and a passive father, he had been desperate to prove his worth academically and professionally. The need to prove his worth had been less urgent, it turned out, during his marriage; but with the loss of his wife and the difficulties of managing his career while functioning as a single parent, the old insecurities returned. Pointing out the various similarities between his current affective state and what he could remember of his childhood was extremely helpful to him. Once he caught on to the pervasive contamination of the experience of his current life by the organized residues of his past, he began to feel better, in part because he was able to deal with current situations objectively and not as threats to his very existence. His personality changed as he became less ingratiating and overanxious and more appropriate in dealing with his social and professional affairs.

Although I did not confront the patient by disputing what he was feeling, I did show him how he was repeating an old pattern in exquisite detail in his current life. He was thus able to arrive fairly quickly at a different vantage from which to view his existence. His affective responses and behavior had been ego syntonic, and I believe it would have been an error to dwell with him on the painful issues of his early life now being reexperienced without providing for the establishment of a therapeutic split between an observing ego and the manifestations of his pathogenic schema.

It is often said, even by those who do not consider themselves self psychologists, that Kohut's contribution lies in his emphasis on empathy. Muslin (1985) put it particularly well: "Kohut's insistence on prolonged empathic immersion into the *experience* of the patient—away from the external behaviors and preformed theories including theories of self psychology—is perhaps of all his contributions the central one" (p. 203). Similarly, in a study on psychoanalytic listening, Schwaber (1983) wrote that in reading Kohut's clinical material it became apparent to her "if one sifted beyond the nosological and theoretical issues he raised, that what Kohut had described was a shift in his own listening stance which enabled him to hear the emergence of different phenomena and even of previously hidden transference formations" (p. 380). Schwaber distinguished between the two separate views of reality in the analytic situation, one held by the analyst and the psychic reality of the patient. Drawing on the work of others, she presented several examples in which the analyst had failed to seek out, hear, and respect the patient's reality but instead had imposed his own reality. In these instances, the analyst made inferential leaps consistent with a priori assumptions and theoretical beliefs. There was a lack of appreciation or, put another way, empathic immersion in the patient's reality. The analyses of these patients were harmed by these empathic failures, and very probably important transference meanings were missed.

In these examples, the analysts responded to single or discrete bits of material, for example, the patient's expression of rage after 40 minutes of silence, without relating the patient's affect and behavior to a precipitating stimulus or wider theme or pattern. Thus, in the summary of her article Schwaber wrote:

> Although such technical precepts as—not to reality test, not to impose one's own perspective, values, or theoretical framework—emphasize the primacy of psychic realty as our clinical purview, analytic listening has betrayed an outlook which remains steeped in a hierarchical two-reality view. The analyst, even as silent arbiter of whether or not distortion has taken place, whether an *event*—immediate or past—is fact or fantasy, is in the implicit position of holding the more "objective" view, incurring the risk thereby of subtly, if not overtly, guiding the patient in accordance with this view [pp. 390–391; italic's added].

The analyst whose work is guided by the schema model would not likely impose his view or act as a silent arbiter concerning the reality of a particular event. A particular event can, and generally does, have many significances, just as an infinite number of lines can pass through a single point; with many derivatives or events there is the possibility of discerning an underlying structure. And Schwaber, along with Kohut, is certainly correct in stressing that it is how the patient experiences an event that is all important. This assertion is entirely consistent with treatment guided by the schema model.

For example, a woman, about 40 years old, married, and the mother of two young children, accepted part-time work in the production of a series of radio shows. The patient was in comfortable circumstances and though the pay was low said she was glad to have the work because the hours were flexible and it gave her a chance to do something interesting while not neglecting her children. She was exceptionally proficient in this work and was given additional duties. Increasing success and recognition stimulated phallic competitive fantasies that found expression in her relationship with her husband and in the analytic transference.

One morning she came to her analytic hour enraged. She had learned that the niece of one of the two women running the company had been hired as a full-time assistant producer. The patient felt that this simply was not fair; this "young kid" was just out of college and would probably be paid $30,000 a year. This was nepotism! Didn't I think she had a right to be angry? The circumstances of this event and the patient's reaction to it brought to mind her rivalry with her only sibling, a younger sister, for their mother's affection; this had been an established theme in the patient's analysis. I asked her if she thought that her strong reaction to this event might not have to do with the sister. The patient laughed and began to point out the similarities between her childhood family and the current situations. This new employee, she realized, even had a name strikingly similar to, and often mistakenly substituted for, the unusual name given the sister. The patient decided that there was nothing to do until it came time to renegotiate her contract, and the situation was for the time being resolved.

In the handling of this event, a great deal of material was gathered, and I inferred that given the patient's pathogenic schema her reaction to the news of the hiring of the new employee had been determined to a significant degree by her unresolved relationship with the sister. I did not confront her with this interpretation; instead I offered it for her contemplation. Two realities were involved, but they were both the patient's own. On one hand, she had perceived and reacted to the event of the hiring of this young woman from the perspective of an organized residue from her traumatic past; on the other hand, she was able to see the situation from the perspective of her current life. It did not occur to me to consider what an appropriate reaction should be.

This is not to say that an analyst whose work is guided by the schema model is thereby insulated from inferential leaps or empathic failures. It does, however, follow from the model that the analyst's function is to listen to the patient and determine from the transference, dreams, and other material the shape and content of the pathogenic residues of the patient's past and to acquaint the patient with this anachronistic organization. The exploration of the patient's mental experience is central to this task.

CHAPTER NINE

◄ ►

A Note on Self-Analysis and Some Questions Frequently Asked About the Schema Model

Although there is no mainstream literature on self-analysis and no generally accepted technique for this procedure, I have found that my own attempts at self-analysis have been significantly facilitated by the adoption of a schema model. In the past, if some strong emotion were stirred, I would think in terms of taming the instincts and what to do about the particular troublesome feeling or impulse I was experiencing. Now I tend to look for configurations rather than concentrating on the drive derivative. I have found that this enables me to find perspective, to separate old scenarios from the current reality.

For example, I had a dream in which I felt frustrated by and furious with a white-haired woman who appeared to be in her 60s. Her appearance and the vague sense that she was wearing something black with a white collar quickly brought to mind the waitress who had served my lunch in the members' restaurant of an art museum the previous day. I remembered that I had been annoyed by the slow service, and that a couple who had come in after me had been served before me. As I recalled the incident, the dining area I habitually used was full and I was ushered into another room. The waitress seemed a bit cool to me, perhaps, I thought, because although she had seen me in the restaurant often, I had not been her customer. By contrast she welcomed warmly the couple, principally the man, who came in after me. I felt annoyed by the fuss she made over him.

That this server of food had seemed cool to me but had

greeted the man who had followed me as an old favorite brought to mind my reactions to the birth of my only sibling, my brother: As I thought back to the time surrounding his birth the affects associated with those memories were strong and poignant, similar to, but sharper than, those I had experienced at lunch the previous day. Other memories of childhood having the theme of deprivation came into consciousness with their associated painful affects. Reflecting on these memories and the dream gave me a perspective in which my current life situation became, it seemed, clearly separated from my hurtful experience as a little boy. I could look back and understand that my parents had intended no harm in having a second child and that other incidents were inadvertent or understandable from the vantage of adulthood.

Such self-analytic ''sessions'' uncover freeze-frames of childhood with their traumatic situations and events, the reactions to these traumata, and the associated affects. In self-analysis, as in therapy, such experiences have the effect of separating the ego from the pathogenic residue, a therapeutic splitting. Subjectively, one is enabled to look back at childhood incidents or chunks of one's childhood from the vantage of maturity and to allow this material to flow into or flood consciousness. Such mixing of warded-off material with the more mature sector of the mind leads to a working over of the warded-off material and ultimately to integration and resolution or, more abstractly, assimilation and accommodation.

Some Questions Frequently Asked About the Schema Model

In this last section, we shall deal with some questions that have been raised in response to presentations of the schema model. In doing so, we shall be going over territory already traversed but in a less formal, more personal voice. Questions were selected from among the many asked at a grand rounds of the psychiatry department of Jefferson Medical College in January 1990; the presentation consisted of a few introductory remarks about the current status of psychoanalytic theory, followed by a brief description of the model and much of the information in Chapter Four.

Q: Would you take some clinical situation and describe how a therapist using a drive-defense model might approach it and how you would approach it within the context of the schema model?

A: Let's take the student athlete (Chapter Four) as our example, specifically his difficulty playing against undergraduates on the varsity team while pursuing graduate studies in Philadelphia. I think that therapists whose work is guided by the structural model would think in terms of a conflict involving instinctual drive derivatives arising from the id's being defended against by mechanisms of the ego. Such a therapist would understand that underlying the inability to play, really a conversion symptom, is the impulse to torture or kill his brother; the inhibition prevents the acting out of this crime and provides punishment in the form of defeat and humiliation. Accordingly, he might say something along the lines of you wish to murder your brother or you are afraid of your murderous feelings toward your brother, which are displaced onto your opponent; since you cannot permit yourself to carry out such a deed you must lose.

A therapist whose work is guided by the schema model would think the game situation not simply a matter of drive derivative opposed by a mechanism of defense but would understand that a current life situation is being cognitively processed as though the patient were back in second grade, living with his parents and his despised kid brother. The patient wishes to exact vengeance on this sibling who deprived him of his mother's exclusive devotion but fears that if he goes too far his father will beat him mercilessly and, if he survived the beating, cast him from the family. The patient did consciously imagine that if he won a particular international tournament he would be shunned by his family and be left alone in the cold.

The interventions of such a therapist would be aimed at helping the patient separate the the reenactment of childhood scenarios from the reality of practicing with or playing against fellow university students with whom he had no special relationships or animosity toward. The drive-defense approach seems focused on the instinctual drive and aimed at helping the patient do something with his aggression—tame it, release it, redirect it; the schema model approach is aimed at helping the patient become aware that some freeze-frame from his traumatic past is being reexperienced and is distorting and disrupting his ability to deal with his current relationships and life situations.

Q: In your presentation you do not seem to make a special point of transference. Does the schema model downplay the importance of transference and the transference neurosis especially when compared with more classical views?

A: Since the phenomenon we call transference is understood according to the schema model as the product of the assimilation of persons in current life into roles and relationships originally created by the important figures of childhood, it is fair to say that transference is central to the model. Transference is ubiquitous. The art history student (Chapter Four) had a transference to her professor, whom she perceived and reacted to as she had in childhood toward her father. She had a brother transference to the male student in her class on women in the history of art. These are extratherapeutic transferences. The student athlete manifested transferences toward me when he withheld material about his sexual behavior lest I tease or criticize him and when he stormed out of sessions when he felt that I was not empathically tuned in to his feelings and experience.

I do differ with those analysts who insist that a sine qua non of a properly conducted analysis is the development of a transference neurosis, by which is signified the replacement of the patient's psychoneurosis by a new neurosis wherein the regressed neurotic conflicts are experienced in large measure, if not exclusively, in the analytic relationship. Many analysts see transference everywhere, and some advocate making only transference interpretations. Yet all the participants in a panel on the then current concept of the transference neurosis held in

Boston in 1969 found that many patients, some of whom did quite well, did not develop transference neuroses. (The individual papers by Blum, Calef, Harley, Loewald, and Weinshel were published in 1971.) Indeed, Harley observed that there is considerable variability in the intensity and consistency of transference manifestations in her cases, and she noted ". . . the common observation that those patients who cathect the analyst with extreme and relatively constant intensity are not infrequently those whose illnesses encompass early and severe ego disturbances" (p. 28). Though classical transference neuroses do occur, often it is a mistake to consider them a necessary component of successful analyses. The couch should not be a procrustean bed.

Q: According to the schema model, is there a real relationship between the patient and the analyst?

A: Yes. Relationships, like everything else experienced by the patient, are the result of forces of the activity of the ego and of sequestered organizations. Since by definition the ego is that part of the mind that perceives objectively and behaves adaptively, the contribution of the ego to the relationship with the analyst must be considered real. The question suggests that there is a point of view that asserts that there is no real relationship with the analyst, that everything is transference. This cannot be. As the patient resolves his transference, his assessment of the analyst is less distorted and more objective. The relationship, thus freed of transference contaminants, does indeed become more real.

Q: Is therapy that is guided by the schema model more ego supportive than classical psychoanalysis?

A: This monograph is about a model, a conceptualization of how the mind is organized, not about a therapy per se; yet therapeutic principles may be inferred from the model. Since therapists of whatever persuasion, by virtue of their individual personalities, vary a great deal in the support they provide, only factors deriving from theory apply to a consideration of this question. Therapies derived from the schema model do provide support in that interventions are addressed to the objective, adaptive part of the patient, the ego. The same may also be said of therapies guided by the structural model, wherein the ego is regarded as the central executive aspect of the mind mediating among the demands of the drives, the superego, and external reality. It is also true that whatever the therapy, for patients with prephallic issues the analytic situation may function as a holding environment (Winnicott, 1965). The functions of the therapist are clear: to listen, to understand, and to impart the understanding so gained to the patient. I would say, then, that therapies guided by the schema model do differ from those which are draconian in their emphasis on silence and deprivation.

Q: Does the schema model approach encourage intellectualization? And are patients able to sense the existence of these pathogenic organizations?

A: The questions are taken together because they are about the polarities of the same continuum. A patient's tendency to employ intellectualization as a defense is encouraged by a technique, whatever the model, that countenances abstract terminology and theory in the therapeutic dialogue. One does well to keep the focus on the patient's experience and experience-near conceptualizations, avoiding theoretical leaps such as hybrid concepts (Slap and Levine, 1978), which combine experiential elements with hypothetical constructs, for example, fear of the loss of ego boundaries.

With time, patients often are able to sense the actuality of their pathological schemas. For example, an internist running a hospital unit became aware during a crisis that he related to a finicky, critical administrator as though she were his mother and that he related to this woman's superior as he did to his father; he related to the doctor who had preceded him in his current position as he had to his older brother, and he was both protective and resentful of subordinates, as he had been to his younger siblings. He was able to grasp that in the work situation he was reliving his childhood family life, with all the old concerns, conflicts, and affects. With this realization he was able to move out of this mode into one in which he was able to perceive the situation objectively and deal with matters adaptively without tension or other symptoms. In the course of treatment, these discoveries occurred many times as part of the working through process.

Pathogenic schemas are not theoretical constructs. The elements that constitute these organizations—traumatic impressions and situations, reactive fantasies, and associated affects—are all capable of being experienced and often are available to consciousness. They are not obvious either to patients or to therapists because some elements and the linkages between elements are unconscious. For the therapist trying to put the underlying configuration together as he pays attention to the patient's history, current material, and derivatives of his conflicts, it is a matter of connecting the dots.

Two additional questions that have been raised by other audiences might usefully be taken up here. First, *if you do away with the id, where will the energy to drive the psychic apparatus come from*? The answer is that the schema model does not do away with the id; both the unitary schema and the sequestered schema are understood to be intersystemic. The id, however conceptualized, is thus understood to be represented in both schemas, albeit the term has practically disappeared from psychoanalytic discourse. It may be that some who have raised this question are confusing psychic energy with physiological processes. We see no reason to assume that the physiological basis of ego and superego functioning relies on energies supplied by the id. The second question is closely related to the the first: *doesn't the schema model do away with the drives* ? Again, because both the sequestered schema and the unitary schema are organizations made up in part of elements that, by virtue of their functions, are drive derivatives, it is clear that the schema model does not do away with drive concepts.

The implications of the schema model do give rise to other sorts of questions. For example, are schemas essentially reactive to events, or are schemas active in the sense of seeking stimulus aliment or nutriment? What makes some schemas easily susceptible to the erosion of their power while others seem indelible? Such questions do not reflect a weakness of the model; rather, it is a strength that the model can generate new and significant problems for investigation. Since the model provides a link to cognitive psychology, the possibility exists that it may provide the basis for fruitful interdisciplinary study.

Indeed, a number of investigators working independently have evolved theories that seem to converge on the concept that schematic templates determine behavior. For example, Luborsky (1977; Levine and Luborsky, 1981) has been working on the core conflictual relationship theme for a decade. Teller and Dahl (1986), working with tapes of psychoanalytic sessions, have studied frames that appear repeatedly in free association. Lewis (1983, pp. 139–140) has called attention to the relevance of script theory for psychoanalysis. She cites Tomkins (1978) who, employing the concept of scenes and a variant of the script concept similar to the schema as here conceptualized, has elaborated a theory of personality structure, development, and dynamics that appears to be compatible with the genetic and dynamic points of view of the psychoanalytic literature. Carlson (1981) has applied Tomkins's script theory clinically in a study indicating this compatibility with psychoanalytic theory, albeit the methodology of her study and the intensity and duration of contact with the subject falls far short of a psychoanalytic investigation. Abelson (1981), also discussed by Lewis, conceives of the script in broader terms; he sees it as a form of a schema that embodies knowledge of stereotyped event sequences. In his view, the script concept has the potential for unifying central notions in learning, developmental, clinical, social, and cognitive psychology. As a consequence, his contributions are less likely to be of immediate interest to those whose work is primarily clinical. Yet his findings are interesting for their potential for indicating bridges between psychoanalysis and general psychology.

References

Abelson, R. P. (1981), Psychological status of the script concept. *Amer. Psychol.*, 36:715–729.

American Psychiatric Association (1980). *Diagnostic and Statistical Manual of Mental Disorders*, Third Edition. Washington, DC: American Psychiatric Association.

Apfelbaum, B. (1965), Ego psychology, psychic energy, and the hazards of quantitative explanation in psychoanalytic theory. *Internat. J. Psycho-Anal.*, 46:168–182.

Arlow, J. A. (1963). Conflict, regression, and symptom formation *Internat. J. Psychoanal.*, 44:12–22.

_____ (1969a). Unconscious fantasy and disturbances of conscious experience. *Psychoanal. Quart.*, 38:1–27.

_____ (1969b). Fantasy, memory, and reality testing. *Psychoanal. Quar.*, 38:28–51.

_____ Brenner, C. (1964). *Psychoanalytic Concepts and the Structural Theory*. New York: International Universities Press.

Atwood, G. E . & Stolorow, R. D. (1984). *Structures of Subjectivity: Explorations in Psychoanalytic Phenomenology*. Hillsdale, NJ: The Analytic Press.

Bartlett, F. C. (1932). *Remembering: A Study in Experimental and Social Psychology*. Cambridge, UK: Cambridge University Press.

Beck, A. T. (1967). *Depression: Clinical, Experimental, and Theoretical Aspects*. New York: Harper & Row.

_____ (1976). *Cognitive Therapy and the Emotional Disorders*. New York: International Universities Press.

Beres, D. & Joseph, E. (1970). The concept of mental representation in psychoanalysis. *Internat. J. Psycho Anal.*, 51:1–9.

Blaney, P. H. (1986). Affect and memory: A review. *Psycholog. Bull.* 99:229–246.

Bliss, E. L. (1986). *Multiple Personality Disorders and Hypnosis.* New York: Oxford University Press.

Blum, H. P. (1971). On the conception and development of the transference neurosis. *J. Amer. Psychoanal. Assn.*, 19:41–53.

Bornstein, M. (1984). Perceptual Development. In: *Developmental Psychology: An Advanced Textbook*, ed. M. Bornstein & M. Lamb. Hillsdale, NJ: Lawrence Erlbaum Associates, pp. 81–126.

Bower, F. H. & Cohen, P. R. (1982). Emotional influences in memory and thinking: Data and theory. In: *Affect and Cognition,* ed. M. S. Clarke & S. T. Fiske. Hillsdale, NJ: Lawrence Erlbaum Associates, pp. 241–331.

Brenner, C. (1974). On the nature and development of affects: a unified theory. *Psychoanal. Quart.* 43:532–555.

——— (1979). Working alliance, therapeutic alliance, and transference. *J. Amer. Psychoanal. Assn.* 27 (Suppl.):137–157.

Breuer, J. & Freud, S. (1893–1895). Studies on hysteria. *Standard Edition*, 2. London: Hogarth Press, 1955.

Calef, V. (1971). On the current concept of the transference neurosis. *J. Amer. Psychoanal. Assn.* 19:22–25, 89–97.

Carlson, R. (1981). Studies in script theory: I. Adult analogs of childhood nuclear scene. *J. Personal. Soc. Psychol.*, 40:501–510.

Cantor, N. & Mischel, W. (1979). Prototypes in person perception, In: *Advances in Experimental Social Psychology*, Vol. 12, ed. L. Berkowitz. New York: Academic Press.

——— & Schwartz, J. (1982). "A Prototype analysis of psychological situations," *Cog. Psychol.*, 14:45–77.

Curtis, H. C. (1979). Concept of the therapeutic alliance: Implications for the "widening space." *J. Amer. Psychoanal. Assn.*, 27 (Suppl.): 159–191.

Fenichel, O. (1941), *Problems of Psychoanalytic Technique*. New York: Psychoanalytic Quarterly.

Fiske, S. (1982). Schema-triggered affect: Application to social perception. In: *Affect and Cognition,* ed. M. S. Clarke & S. T. Fiske. Hillsdale, NJ: Lawrence Erlbaum Associates, pp. 55–78.

Flavell, J. H. (1963). *The Developmental Psychology of Jean Piaget*. New York: Van Nostrand.

Frattaroli, E. J. (1984). The current status of the structural theory. Report on the discussion group meeting, Dec. 19. Unpublished.

Freud, A. (1936). *The Ego and the Mechanisms of Defense in the Writings of Anna Freud*, Vol. 2. New York: International Universities Press.

_____ (1965). *Normality and Pathology in Childhood: Assessments of Development*. New York: International Universities Press.

Freud, S. (1895). Project for a scientific psychology. *Standard Edition*, 1:295–397. London: Hogarth Press, 1966.

_____ (1896). Heredity and the aetiology of the neuroses. *Standard Edition*, 3:141–161. London: Hogarth Press.

_____ (1898). Sexuality in the aetiology of the neurosis. *Standard Edition*. 3:263–285. London: Hogarth Press, 1962.

_____ (1900). The interpretation of dreams. *Standard Edition*, 4 & 5. London: Hogarth Press, 1953.

_____ (1905). Three essays on the theory of sexuality. *Standard Edition*, 7:135–243. London: Hogarth Press, 1953.

_____ (1906). My views on the part played by sexuality in the aetiology of the neurosis. *Standard Edition*, 7:271–299. London: Hogarth Press, 1953.

_____ (1909). Analysis of a phobia in a five-year-old boy. *Standard Edition*, 10:3–152. London: Hogarth Press, 1955.

_____ (1912). Recommendations to physicians practising psychoanalysis. *Standard Edition*, 12:109–120. London: Hogarth Press.

_____ (1914). On narcissism: An introduction. *Standard Edition*, 14:73–102. London: Hogarth Press, 1957. London: Hogarth Press, 1957.

_____ (1915). The unconscious. *Standard Edition*, 14: 166–204. London: Hogarth Press, 1957.

_____ (1916–1917). Introductory lectures on psychoanalysis. *Standard Edition*, 15 & 16. London: Hogarth Press, 1963.

_____ (1920). Beyond the pleasure principle. *Standard Edition*, 18:7–64. London: Hogarth Press, 1955.

_____ (1923). The ego and the id. *Standard Edition*, 19:12–66. London: Hogarth Press, 1961.

_____ (1925a). A note on the mystic writing pad. *Standard Edition*, 19: London: Hogarth Press, 1961.

_____ (1925b). Some additional notes on dream interpretation as a whole. *Standard Edition*, 19: 125–140. London: Hogarth Press, 1961.

_____ (1926). Inhibitions, symptoms and anxiety. *Standard Edition*, 20: 87–172. London: Hogarth Press, 1959.

_____ (1927). Fetishism. *Standard Edition* 21: 149–167. London: Hogarth Press, 1961.

_____ (1928). Dostoevsky and parricide. *Standard Edition* 21:177–194. London: Hogarth Press, 1961.

_____ (1931). The expert opinion in the Halsmann case. *Standard Edition* 21: 251–253, London: Hogarth Press, 1961.

_____ (1933). New introductory lectures on psychoanalysis. *Standard Edition*, 22: 5–182. London: Hogarth Press, 1964.

_____ (1937). Analysis terminable and interminable. *Standard Edition*, 23:216–253. London: Hogarth Press, 1964.

_____ (1939). Moses and monotheism. *Standard Edition*, 23: 1–137. London: Hogarth Press, 1964.

_____ (1940). Outline of psychoanalysis. *Standard Edition*, 23: 144–207. London: Hogarth Press, 1964.

Furst, S. S. ed. (1967), *Psychic Trauma*. New York: Basic Books.

Gay, P. (1988). *Freud: A Life for Our Time*. New York: Norton.

Gill, M. M. (1963). Topography and systems in psychoanalytic theory. *Psychological Issues,* Monogr. 10. New York: International Universities Press.

Ginsburg, H. P. & Opper, S. (1988). *Piaget's Theory of Intellectual Development*. New York: Prentice Hall.

Greenacre, P. (1954). The role of transference. *J. Amer. Psychoanal. Assn.*, 2:671–684.

_____ (1967). The influence of infantile trauma on genetic patterns. In: *Emotional Growth*, Vol. 1. New York: International Universities Press, 1971.

Greenson, R. (1965), The working alliance and the transference neurosis. *Psychoanal. Quart.*, 34:151–181.

_____ Wexler, M. (1969), The non-transference relationship in the psychoanalytic situation. *Internat. J. Psycho-Anal.*, 50:27–40.

Guntrip, H. *Schizoid Phenomena, Object Relations and the Self*. New York: International Universities Press.

Harley, M. (1971). The current status of the transference neurosis in children. *J. Amer. Psychoanal. Assn.*, 19:26–40.

Hartmann, E. L. (1973). *The Functions of Sleep*. New Haven, CT: Yale University Press.

Hartmann, H. (1958). *The Problem of Adaptation*. New York: International Universities Press.

_____ (1964). *Essays on Ego Psychology* New York: International Universities Press.

Hartmann, H., Kris, E. & Loewenstein, R. M. (1946). Comments on the formation of psychic structure. *The Psychoanalytic Study of the Child*, 2:11–38. New York: International Universities of Press.

_____ _____ _____ (1949). Notes on the theory of aggression. *The Psychoanalytic Study of the Child*, 3/4:9–36. New York: International Universities Press.

Higgins, E. T., Rholes, W. S. & Jones, C. R. (1977). Category accessibility and impression formation. *J. Exper. Soc. Psychol.,* 13: 141–154.

Horowitz, M. (1971). The compulsion to repeat trauma. *J. Nerv. Ment. Dis.*, 153: 32–40.

_____ (1977a). Cognitive and interactive aspects of splitting. *Amer. J. Psychiat.*, 134:549–553.

_____ ed. (1977b). *Hysterical Personality*. New York: Aronson.

_____ (1988). *Introduction to Psychodynamics*. New York: Basic Books.

Inderbitzen, L. B. & Levy, S. (1990). Unconscious fantasy, A reconsideration of the concept. *J. Amer. Psychoanal. Assn.*, 38:113–130.

Janet, P. (1906). *The Major Symptoms of Hysteria*. New York: Macmillan, 1920.

Kegan, R. (1982). *The Evolving Self*. Cambridge, MA: Harvard University Press.

Kernberg, O. (1967). Borderline personality organization. *J. Amer. Psychoanal. Assn.*, 15:641–685.

_____ (1974). Contrasting viewpoints regarding the nature and psychoanalytic treatment of narcissistic personalities: A preliminary communication. J. Amer. Psychoanal. Assn., 22:255–267.

_____ (1976). *Object Relations Theory and Clinical Psychoanalysis*. New York: J. Aronson.

Klein, G. S. (1976). *Psychoanalytic Theory: An Explanation of Essentials*. New York: International Universities Press.

Kohut, H. (1971). *The Analysis of the Self.* New York: International Universities Press.

_____ (1984). *How Does Analysis Cure?* ed. A. Goldberg & P. Stepansky. Chicago: University of Chicago Press.

Kovacs, M. & Beck, A. T. (1978). Maladaptive cognitive structures in depression. *Amer. J. Psychiat.,* 135:525–533.

Kuhn, T. S. (1970). *The Structure of Scientific Revolutions.* Chicago: University of Chicago Press.

Levine, F. J. & Luborsky, L. (1981). The core conflictual relationship theme. In: *Object and Self: A Developmental Approach,* ed. S. Tuttman, C. Kaye, & M. Zimmerman. New York: International Universities Press, pp. 521–526.

Lewis, H. B. (1983). *Freud and Modern psychology,* Vol. 2. New York: Plenum.

Lichtenberg, J. (1983). *Psychoanalysis and Infant Research.* Hillsdale, NJ: The Analytic Press.

_____ Slap, J. W. (1973). Notes on the concept of splitting and the defense mechanism of splitting of representations. *J. Amer. Psychoanal. Assn.,* 21:772–787.

_____ _____ (1977). Comments on the General Functioning of the Analyst in the Psychoanalytic Situation. *The Annual of Psychoanalysis,* 5:295–312. New York: International Universities Press.

Linnel, Z. M. (1990). What is mental representation? A study of its elements and how they lead to language. *J. Amer. Psychoanal. Assn..,* 38:131–165.

Loewald, H. W. (1971). The transference neurosis: Comments on the concept and phenomenon. *J. Amer. Psychoanal. Assn.,* 19:67–88.

Luborsky, L. (1977). Measuring a pervasive psychic structure in psychotherapy: The core conflictual relationship there. In: *Communicative Structures and Psychic Structures,* ed. N. Freedman & S. Grand. New York: Plenum, pp. 367–395.

Marcovitz, E. (1963). Panel report on the "Concept of the id." *J. Amer. Psychoanal. Assn.,* 11:151–160.

Muslin, H. L. (1985). *Heinz Kohut: Beyond the pleasure* principle, contributions to psychoanalysis. In: *Beyond Freud,* ed. J. Reppen. Hillsdale, NJ: The Analytic Press, pp. 203–229.

Neubauer, (1967). Trauma and psychopathology. In: *Psychic Trauma,* ed. S. Furst. New York: Basic Books, pp. 85–107.

Nunberg, H. (1948). *Practice and Theory of Psychoanalysis*. New York: International Universities Press.

Paul, I. H. (1967), Studies in remembering. *Psychological Issues*, Monogr. 2. New York; International Universities Press.

Piaget, J. (1926). *The Language and Thought of the Child*. New York: Basic Books.

_____ Inhelder, B. (1969). *The Psychology of the Child*. New York: Basic Books.

Rangell, L. (1967). The metapsychology of psychic trauma. In: *Psychic Trauma*, ed. S. Furst. New York: Basic Books, pp. 51–84.

Reiser, M. S. (1984). *Mind, Body, Brain*. New York: Basic Books.

Rostand, E. (1897). *Cyrano de Bergerac*. New York: Modern Library, 1951.

Sandler, J. (1983). Reflections on some relations between psychoanalytic concepts and psychoanalytic practice. *Internat. J. Psycho-Anal.*, 64:35–45.

Schafer, R. (1968). *Aspects of Internalization*. New York: International Universities Press.

Schank, R. C. & Abelson, R. P. (1977). *Scripts, Plans, Goals, and Understanding*. Hillsdale, NJ: Lawrence Erlbaum Associates.

Schimek, J. G. (1975). A critical re-examination of Freud's concept of unconscious mental representation. *Internat. Rev. Psychoanal.*, 2:171–187.

Schur, M. (1966). *The Id and the Regulatory Principles of Mental Functioning*. New York: International Universities Press.

Schwaber, E. (1983). Psychoanalytic listening and psychic reality. *Internat. Rev. Psychoanal.*, 10: 379–392.

Segal, Z. V. (1988). Appraisal of the self-schema construct in cognitive models of depression. *Psycholog. Bull.*, 103:147–162.

Slap, J. W. (1974). On waking screens. *J. Amer. Psychoanal. Assn.*, 22:844–853.

_____ (1977). On dreaming at sleep onset, *Psychoanal. Quart.*, 46:71–81.

_____ (1979). On nothing and nobody with an addendum on William Hogarth. *Psychoanal. Quart.*, 48:620–627.

_____ (1982). An unusual infantile theory of the origin of the female sex. *Psychoanal. Quart.*, 51:418–420.

_____ (1986). Some problems with the structural model and a remedy. *Psychoanal. Psychol.*, 3:47–58.

——— (1987). Implications for the structural model of Freud's assumptions about perception. *J. Amer. Psychoanal. Assn.*, 35: 629–646.

——— Levine, F. J. (1978). On hybrid concepts in psychoanalysis. *Psychoanal. Quart.*, 47:499–523.

——— Saykin, A. J. (1983). The schema: Basic concept in a nonmetapsychological model of the mind. *Psychoanal. Contemp. Thought*, 6:305–325.

——— ——— (1984). On the nature and the organization of the repressed. *Psychoanal. Inq.*, 4:107–124.

——— Trunnell, E. E. (1987). Reflections on the self state dream. *Psychoanal. Quart.*, 46:251–262.

Solnit, A. & Kris, M. (1967). Trauma and infantile experiences: A longitudinal perspective. In: *Psychic Trauma*, ed. S. Furst. New York: Basic Books, pp. 175–220

Stern, D. (1985). *The Interpersonal World of the Infant*. New York: Basic Books.

Stolorow, R. D. (1978). The concept of psychic structure: Its metapsychological and clinical meanings. *Internat. Rev. Psychoanal., 5:313–320.*

——— Lachmann, F. M. (1986). *Psychoanalysis of Developmental Arrests*. Madison, CT: International Universities Press.

Stone, L. (1961), *The Psychoanalytic Situation*. New York: International Universities Press.

Tarachow, S. (1961). A brief clinical reference to an aesthetic feeling. *Bull. Phila. Assn. Psychoanal.*, 11:129.

Taylor S. E. & Crocker, J. (1980). Schematic bases of social information processing. In: *Social Cognition,* ed. E. T. Higgins, P. M. Herman & M. P. Zanna. Hillsdale, NJ: Lawrence Erlbaum Associates.

Teller, V. & Dahl, H. (1986). The microstructure of free association. *J. Amer. Psychoanal. Assn.*, 34:763—798.

Tomkins, S. (1978). Script theory: Differential magnifications of effects. In: *Nebraska Symposium on Motivation*, Vol. 26, ed. H. E. Howe, Jr. & M. M. Page. Lincoln: University of Nebraska Press, pp. 201–236.

Tulving, E. & Pearlstone, Z. (1966). Availability versus accessibility of information in memory for words. *J. Verbal Learn. & Verbal Beh.,* 5:331–391.

Van der Kolk, B. A. & van der Hart, O. (1989). Pierre Janet and the breakdown of adaptation in psychological trauma, *Amer. J. Psychiat.,* 146:1530–1540.

Wachtel, P. (1980). Transference, schema, and assimilation: The relevance of Piaget to the psychoanalytic theory of transference. *The Annual of Psychoanalysis*, 8:59–76. New York: International Universities Press.

Waelder, R. (1936). The principle of multiple function: Observations on overdetermination. *Psychoanal. Quart.*, 5:45–62.

_____ (1960). *Basic Theory of Psychoanalysis*. New York: International Universities Press.

_____ (1962). Review of S. Hook (Ed.), *Psychoanalysis, scientific method, and philosophy: A symposium. J. Amer. Psychoanal. Assn.*, 10:617–637.

Wallerstein, R. S. (1989). Psychoanalysis and psychotherapy: An historical perspective. Freud Memorial Lecture presented to Philadelphia Association for Psychoanalysis, March 31.

Weinshel, E. M. (1971). The transference of neurosis: A survey of the literature. *J. Amer. Psychoanal. Assn.*, 19:67–88.

Westen, D. (1988). Transference and information processing. *Psycholog. Rev.*, 8:101–180.

Winnicott, D. W. (1965). *The Maturational Processes and the Facilitating Environment*. New York: International Universities Press.

Wolff, Peter H. (1960). *The Developmental Psychologies of Jean Piaget and Psychoanalysis*. New York International Universities Press.

_____ (1966). The causes, controls, and organization of behavior in the neonate. *Psychological Issues*,. Monogr. 5. New York: International Universities Press.

Zetzel, E. R. (1956). Current concepts of transference. *Internat. J. Psycho-Anal.*, 37: 369–378.

_____ (1966). The analytic situation. In: *Psychoanalysis in the Americas*, ed. R. E. Litman. New York: International Universities Press, pp. 86–106.

Author Index

Subject Index